Italian Grammar

Second Edition

by
Marcel Danesi, Ph.D.
Professor of Romance Linguistics, University of Toronto

BARRON'S

BARRON'S EDUCATIONAL SERIES, INC.

All inquiries should be addressed to:
Barron's Educational Series, Inc.
250 Wireless Boulevard
Hauppauge, NY 11788

International Standard Book Number 0-7641-2060-3

Library of Congress Cataloging-in-Publication Data

Danesi, Marcel, 1946–
    Italian grammar / Marcel Danesi.—2nd ed.
      p. cm.
    Includes index.
    ISBN 0-7641-2060-3
     1. Italian language—Grammar.

PC1112 .D35 2002
458.2′421—dc21

                                    2001052832

Printed in China
9 8 7 6

Contents

Parts of Speech

Preface

This book is one of a series of handy grammar reference guides. It is designed for students, businesspeople, and others who want to "brush up" their knowledge of Italian grammar. Actually, this is a crucial stage in the process of learning another language. It gives you the opportunity to reflect upon what you know, to reinforce your skills, to fill in the gaps, to clarify difficult points—in sum, to help you build a more solid linguistic foundation.

Whether you are just beginning your study of Italian or have had some Italian and want to refresh your memory, this book is for you. Previous knowledge has not been taken for granted in these pages; definitions and explanations are concise and clear, and examples use and reuse a core of basic vocabulary.

The main part of this book is divided into four sections: "The Basics," "Parts of Speech," "Special Topics," and "Verb Charts."

- In the "Basics" section you will find a nontechnical and easy-to-follow discussion of Italian sounds, spelling conventions, and word-order patterns.
- In the "Parts of Speech" section you will find the nouns, articles, pronouns, etc. that make up the Italian language.
- The "Special Topics" section contains idiomatic expressions, numbers, synonyms, antonyms, etc.
- The "Verb Charts" section contains a list of common irregular verbs, fully conjugated.

Marcel Danesi, Ph.D.
University of Toronto

How to Use This Book

In the chapters that follow, a numerical decimal system has been used with the symbol § in front of it. This was done so that you may find quickly and easily the reference to a particular point in Italian grammar when you use the index. For example, if you look up the entry "prepositions" in the index, you will find the reference given as §10. Sometimes, additional § reference numbers are given when the entry you consulted is mentioned in other areas in the chapter §.

You can read this book as if it were a "story"—the "grammatical story" of the Italian language. You should start reading from page one and work your way through it a little at a time. The book is designed to be sequential and coherent. There are also cross-references to guide you along the way, in the event you may have forgotten something.

By the end of the "story," you will be in a position to grasp the fundamentals of the Italian language.

You can also use this book as a reference manual, using the table of contents and the index to guide you to the areas of grammar on which you need information. As such, this book can be valuable as a tool in Italian language courses and as a general "vademecum" of Italian grammar.

New Features

This second edition of *Italian Grammar* has several new features that further enhance its usefulness.

- Many of the sections have been expanded and updated in terms of information and vocabulary.
- Italian terms for grammatical notions have been added throughout.
- Tips for studying the more troublesome grammatical aspects have been interspersed throughout.
- Charts have been revised and laid out much more clearly.
- Main features of grammar and vocabulary are highlighted in color so that you can spot them right away. So too are the many tips interspersed throughout. The titles of other relevant lists are highlighted as well to indicate that they contain important information.

The Basics

§1.
Guide to Italian Sounds and Spelling

§1.1   WHAT ARE VOWELS AND CONSONANTS?

> *Le vocali e le consonanti*

There are two kinds of basic sounds in any language: *vowels* and *consonants*.

> *Vowels* are produced by air passing out through the mouth without being blocked. The letters that represent these sounds are: *a, e, i, o, u*.

> *Consonants*, on the other hand, are produced by blockage (partial or complete) of the air. The remaining alphabet letters are used to represent consonant sounds: *b, c, d*, etc.

§1.2   VOWELS

Italian vowels should not cause you any problems.

Alphabet Letters	Sounds	Examples
a	Similar to the *a* sound in "father," or to the exclamation "ah!"	*casa* / house *acqua* / water
e	Similar to the *e* sound in "bet," or to the exclamation "eh!"	*bene* / well *esame* / exam
i	Similar to the *i* sound in "machine," or to the exclamation "eeh!"	*vini* / wines *indirizzi* / addresses
o	Similar to the *o* sound in "sorry," or to the exclamation "oh!"	*otto* / eight *oro* / gold
u	Similar to the *oo* sound in "boot," or to the exclamation "ooh!"	*uva* / grapes *gusto* / taste

Speakers in various parts of Italy pronounce *e* and *o* differently. In some parts, these vowels are pronounced with the mouth relatively more open. In others, they are pronounced with the mouth relatively more closed. In many areas, however, *both* pronunciations are used.

To get an idea of what this means, consider how the *a* in "tomato" is pronounced in North America. In some areas, it is pronounced like the *a* in "father." In other areas, it is pronounced like the *a* in "pay." However, whether it is pronounced one way or the other, no one will have much difficulty understanding that the word is "tomato." This is exactly what happens in the case of Italian *e* and *o*.

The letter *i* stands for the semivowel sounds similar to those represented by the *y* in "yes" and "say."

The *i* pronounced like	The *i* pronounced like
y in "yes"	*y* in "say"
ieri / yesterday	*mai* / ever, never
piatto / plate	*poi* / then

This pronunciation feature occurs when the *i* is next to another vowel and both are pronounced rapidly together. If there is a slight pause between the two vowels, then pronounce *i* in its normal way as in the word *zio* (uncle).

Similarly, the letter *u* stands for the semivowel sounds represented by the *w* in "way" and "how."

The *u* pronounced like	The *u* pronounced like
w in "way"	*w* in "how"
uomo / man	*causa* / cause
buono / good	*laurea* / degree (university)

Once again, this feature occurs when the *u* is next to another vowel and both are pronounced rapidly together.

§1.3 CONSONANTS

The following Italian consonants should cause you few problems:

Alphabet Letters	Sounds	Examples
b	Identical to the *b* sound in "boy."	*bello* / beautiful *bravo* / good
d	Identical to the *d* sound in "day." This is true even when followed by *r*; in English, the tongue is raised a bit more: "drop."	*dopo* / after *ladro* / thief
f	Identical to the *f* sound in "fun."	*forte* / strong *frutta* / fruit

Alphabet Letters	Sounds	Examples
l	Identical to the *l* sound in "love." However, in English, the back of the tongue is raised a bit more: "bill."	*latte* / milk *alto* / tall
m	Identical to the *m* sound in "more."	*matita* / pencil *mondo* / world
n	Identical to the *n* sound in "nose."	*naso* / nose *nono* / ninth
p	Identical to the *p* sound in "price."	*porta* / door *prezzo* / price
q	Identical to the *q* sound in "quick." It is always followed by *u*.	*quanto* / how much *quinto* / fifth
r	Like a "rolled" *r* sound (as in some Scottish dialects). Pronounced with a few flips of tongue against the upper gums.	*rosso* / red *raro* / rare
t	Like the *t* sound in "fat" (with the tongue against the upper teeth).	*tardi* / late *tu* / you
v	Identical to the *v* sound in "vine."	*vino* / wine *vero* / true

The following consonants are pronounced in different ways, as explained in the chart:

Alphabet Letters	Sounds	Examples
c	Represents the *k* sound as in "kit" and "cat." Used in front of *a*, *o*, *u*, and any consonant.	Before *a*, *o*, *u*: *cane* / dog *come* / how *cuore* / heart Before any consonant: *classe* / class *cravatta* / tie
ch	Represents the same *k* sound. Used in front of *e* and *i*.	*che* / what *chi* / who *chiesa* / church
c	Represents the *ch* sound as in "church." Used in front of *e* and *i*.	*cena* / dinner *cinema* / movies
ci	Represents the *ch* sound in front of *a*, *o*, *u*.	*ciao* / hi, bye *cioccolata* / chocolate
g	Represents the *g* sound as in "good." Used in front of *a*, *o*, *u*, and any consonant.	Before *a*, *o*, *u*: *gatto* / cat *gola* / throat *guanto* / glove Before any consonant: *gloria* / glory *grande* / big, large
gh	Represents the same *g* sound. Used in front of *e* and *i*.	*spaghetti* / spaghetti *ghiaccio* / ice

Alphabet Letters	Sounds	Examples
g	Represents the *j* sound as in "just." Used in front of *e* and *i*.	*gente* / people *giro* / turn, tour
gi	Represents the same *j* sound. Used in front of *a, o, u*.	*giacca* / jacket *giorno* / day *giugno* / June
sc	Represents the sound sequence *sk* in front of *a, o, u*, or any consonant.	*scala* / staircase *scopa* / broom *scuola* / school *scrivere* / to write
sch	Represents the same *sk* sequence in front of *e* and *i*.	*scherzo* / prank *schifo* / disgust
sc	Represents the *sh* sound in front of *e* and *i*.	*scena* / scene *sciocco* / unsalted, flavorless
sci	Represents the same *sh* sound in front of *a, o, u*.	*sciopero* / labor strike *sciupare* / to waste

The sound represented by *gli* is similar to the *lli* in "million":

figlio / son
luglio / July

The sound represented by *gn* is similar to the *ny* of "canyon":

sogno / dream
giugno / June

The letter *s* can stand for both the *s* sound in "sip" or the *z* sound in "zip." The *z* sound occurs before *b, d, g, l, m, n, r, v*; otherwise, the *s* sound is used.

Examples

s-sound	z-sound
sapone / soap	*sbaglio* / mistake
sete / thirst	*svegliarsi* / to wake up
specchio / mirror	*slittare* / to slide

When *s* occurs between vowels, either sound may be used.

The letter *z* stands for the *ts* sound in "cats" or the *ds* sound in "lads":

The letter *h* does not represent any sound. It is like the silent *h* of "hour":

ho (pronounced "oh!") / I have

Any one of these consonants can have a corresponding double articulation. The pronunciation of double consonants simply lasts twice as long as that of the corresponding single consonant.

Examples

Single Consonant	Corresponding Double Consonant
fato / fate	*fatto* / fact
caro / dear	*carro* / cart
pala / shovel	*palla* / ball
sono / I am	*sonno* / sleep

§1.4 STRESS

L'accento

Knowing where to put the stress, or main accent, on an Italian word is not always easy, but you can always look up a word you are unsure of in a dictionary that indicates stress. Here are some general guidelines:

> In many words, the stress falls on the next-to-last syllable. You can identify most syllables easily because they contain a vowel.

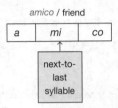

amico / friend

a	mi	co

next-to-last syllable

But be careful! This is not always the case.

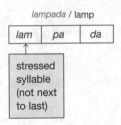

lampada / lamp

lam	pa	da

stressed syllable (not next to last)

> **Tip**
>
> Assume, in general, that the accent falls on the second-to-last syllable. Statistically speaking, this is the best strategy, since most Italian words are accented in this way.
>
> But, to be absolutely sure, always check a good dictionary.

Some words show an accent mark on the final vowel. This is, of course, where you put the stress.

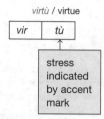

virtù / virtue

| *vir* | *tù* |

stress
indicated
by accent
mark

The accent mark in Italian can always be made to slant to the left (*à*). However, in words ending in *-ché*, it normally slants to the right.

Examples

città / city
gioventù / youth
perché (or *perchè*) / why, because
benché (or *benchè*) / although

§1.5 SPELLING CONVENTIONS

L'ortografia

To spell most Italian words, use the letter-to-sound correspondences described in the previous sections. Italian also uses the same punctuation marks as English (period, comma, semicolon, interrogative mark, exclamation point, etc.).

The Italian alphabet does not have the letters *j, k, w, x, and y*. These are found, however, in words that Italian has borrowed from other languages (primarily English).

Examples

il karatè / karate
il jazz / jazz
il weekend / weekend
lo yacht / yacht
il software / software
l' hardware / hardware

Like English, capital letters are used at the beginning of sentences and to write proper nouns (see §3.1). However, there are a few different conventions worth noting.

The pronoun *io* (I) is not capitalized (unless it is the first word of a sentence).

Vengo anche io. / I'm coming too.

Titles are not usually capitalized.

il professor Verdi / Professor Verdi
la dottoressa Martini / Dr. Martini

Adjectives and nouns referring to languages and nationality are not capitalized.

É un italiano. / He is an Italian.
La lingua spagnola è interessante. / The Spanish language is interesting.

Names of the seasons, months of the year, and days of the week also are not capitalized.

la primavera / Spring
mercoledì / Wednesday
maggio / May

Summaries of Word Order in an Italian Sentence

§2.1 WHAT IS A SENTENCE?

> *Il periodo*

A *sentence* is an organized series of words that allows one to make a statement, ask a question, express a thought, offer an opinion, etc. In writing, a sentence is easily identified because it starts with a capitalized word and ends with either a period, a question mark, or an exclamation mark.

Examples

Quella donna è italiana. / That woman is Italian. (statement)
È italiana, quella donna? / Is that woman Italian? (question)
Penso che quella donna sia italiana. / I think that woman is Italian.
  (thought/opinion)

Notice that a sentence is organized in relation to what you intend to say and how you are going to say it. You cannot put words in just any order!

Jumbled	**Organized**
donna è italiana quella	*Quella donna è italiana.*

Sentences have two basic parts: a *subject* and a *predicate*.

A *subject* is "who" or "what" the sentence is about. It is often the first element in a simple sentence.

Examples

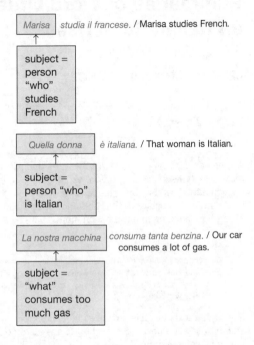

Marisa studia il francese. / Marisa studies French.

subject =
person
"who"
studies
French

Quella donna è italiana. / That woman is Italian.

subject =
person "who"
is Italian

La nostra macchina consuma tanta benzina. / Our car
consumes a lot of gas.

subject =
"what"
consumes too
much gas

But be careful! The subject is not necessarily always the first
word in the sentence.

Examples

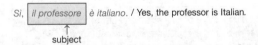

Sì, *il professore* è italiano. / Yes, the professor is Italian.

subject

Consuma tanta benzina | la tua macchina? | / Does your car
                                                    consume a
                                          ↑   lot of gas?
                                        subject

A *predicate* is the remaining part of the sentence. It
provides information about the subject. In many simple
sentences, you will find it after the subject.

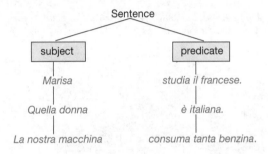

Sentence

| subject | predicate |

Marisa — *studia il francese.*

Quella donna — *è italiana.*

La nostra macchina — *consuma tanta benzina.*

A sentence can have more than one subject or predicate.

Maria	*dice che*	*quella donna*	*è italiana.*
↑	↑	↑	↑
main subject	main predicate	subordinate subject	subordinate predicate

A subject must contain a noun, substantive (anything that can
stand for a noun), noun phrase (see Chapter 3), or pronoun
(see Chapter 7); a predicate must include a verb (see Chapter
8). The parts of speech that make up the subject and predicate are defined and discussed in Chapters 3 to 11.

§2.2 SENTENCES BY FUNCTION

Sentences have specific functions. They allow you to make statements, ask questions, express mood, and so on.

§2.2–1 Affirmative

Il periodo affermativo

An *affirmative* sentence allows you to state or affirm something in a straightforward way.

Examples

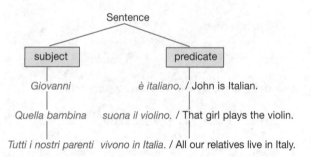

The predicate of affirmative sentences may or may not have an object. An *object* is the noun, substantive, or noun phrase that receives the action, and normally follows a verb. A pronoun can also function as an object.

There are two types of objects: *direct* and *indirect*. These can be identified very easily as follows:

> A noun, substantive, or noun phrase, that directly follows the verb is a *direct object*.

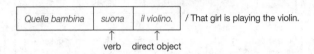

Quella bambina	*suona*	*il violino.*
	↑	↑
	verb	direct object

/ That girl is playing the violin.

> A noun, substantive, or noun phrase, that follows the verb but is introduced by the preposition *a* (to, at) is an *indirect object*.

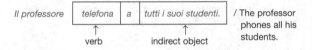

Il professore	*telefona*	*a*	*tutti i suoi studenti.*
	↑		↑
	verb		indirect object

/ The professor phones all his students.

Whether an object is direct or indirect depends on the verb. Some verbs must be followed only by one type of object or the other. Fortunately, most verbs in Italian match their English equivalents when it comes to whether or not a direct or indirect object should follow.

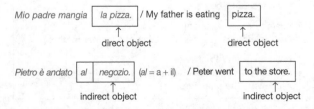

Mio padre mangia | *la pizza.* / My father is eating | pizza.
direct object — direct object

Pietro è andato | *al* | *negozio.* (*al* = a + il) / Peter went | to the store.
indirect object — indirect object

However, there are differences! Here are the most important ones.

Verbs Requiring a Direct Object

ascoltare / to listen (to)
Mia madre ascolta la radio ogni sera. / My mother listens to the radio every evening.

aspettare / to wait (for)
Maria aspetta l'autobus. / Mary is waiting for the bus.

cercare / to search, look (for)
Tina cerca la sua borsa. / Tina is looking for her purse.

One way to remember these differences is to view the Italian verb as "containing" the preposition.

Maria | aspetta | *l'autobus.*
is waiting for

Verbs Requiring an Indirect Object

chiedere / domandare (a) / to ask (someone)
Gino chiede al professore di venire. / Gino asks the professor to come.

telefonare (a) / to phone
Gina telefona a sua madre. / Gina phones her mother.

rispondere (a) / to answer
La studentessa risponde alla domanda. / The student answers the question.

Some verbs can take both kinds of objects.

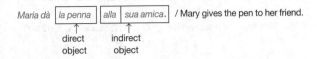

Maria dà | *la penna* | *alla* | *sua amica.* | / Mary gives the pen to her friend.

↑ direct object   ↑ indirect object

As mentioned, an object is not always needed in a sentence.

Examples

Il bambino dorme. / The child is sleeping.
Loro partono domani. / They are leaving tomorrow.

§2.2–2   Negative

> *Il periodo negativo*

To make any sentence negative in Italian, just put *non* before the predicate.

Examples

Affirmative	**Negative**
Maria aspetta l'autobus. / Mary is waiting for the bus.	*Maria non aspetta l'autobus.* / Mary is not waiting for the bus.
Il bambino dorme. / The child is sleeping.	*Il bambino non dorme.* / The child is not sleeping.
Maria mi dà la mela. / Mary gives me the apple.	*Maria non mi dà la mela.* / Mary does not give me the apple.

Notice that the pronoun *mi*, which is still part of the predicate, comes before the verb (see §7.3.1).

"Yes" and "No"

sì / yes
Sì, Gina aspetta il suo amico. / Yes, Gina is waiting for her
  friend.
no / no
No, Gina non aspetta il suo amico. / No, Gina is not waiting for her friend.

---

§2.2–3 Interrogative

Il periodo interrogativo

An interrogative sentence allows you to ask a question. In
writing, it always has a question mark at the end. The two
most common methods of turning an affirmative sentence into
an interrogative one are:

Simply put a question mark at the end. In speaking, the
voice goes up at the end of the sentence as in English.

Examples

Affirmative
Anna cerca il gatto. /
  Ann is looking for the cat.
Il bambino dorme. /
  The child is sleeping.

Interrogative
Anna cerca il gatto? /
  Ann is looking for the cat?
Il bambino dorme? /
  The child is sleeping?

Put the subject at the end of the sentence, adding a
question mark.

Examples

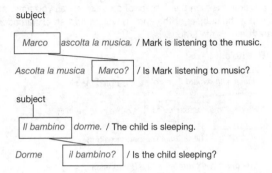

subject

Marco | *ascolta la musica.* / Mark is listening to the music.

Ascolta la musica | *Marco?* / Is Mark listening to music?

subject

Il bambino | *dorme.* / The child is sleeping.

Dorme | *il bambino?* / Is the child sleeping?

Interrogative sentences can also be formed with interrogative adjectives (see §6.4–2) or pronouns (see §7.2). These allow you to ask "what?", "when?", "where?," etc.

Examples

Quale macchina preferisci? / Which car do you prefer?
Come va? / How's it going?

Use either *no?*, *vero?*, or *non è vero?* to seek approval, consent, agreement, etc.

Examples

Giovanni è italiano, no? / John is Italian, isn't he?
Tua madre guida una macchina sportiva, vero? / Your mother drives a sports car, doesn't she?
Lei parla molto bene, non è vero? / She speaks very well, doesn't she?

§2.2–4 Emphatic

To put emphasis on the subject of a sentence, all you have to
do is put the subject at the end. In writing add an exclamation
mark to show the emphasis.

Examples

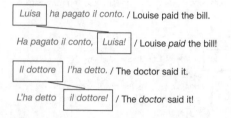

Luisa ha pagato il conto. / Louise paid the bill.

Ha pagato il conto, *Luisa!* / Louise *paid* the bill!

Il dottore l'ha detto. / The doctor said it.

L'ha detto *il dottore!* / The *doctor* said it!

The imperative forms of the verb also add emphasis
(see §8.3).

Anna, paga il conto! / Ann, pay the bill!

§2.3 SENTENCES BY STRUCTURE

Sentences can have a simple or complex structure.

§2.3–1 Simple

A simple sentence has only one (main) subject and one (main)
predicate.

Examples

Alessandro è intelligente. / Alexander is intelligent.
Sara è molto brava. / Sarah is very good.

§2.3–2 Complex

A complex sentence has at least one subordinate, or dependent, clause. A *clause* is a group of related words that

contains a subject and predicate and is part of the main sentence.

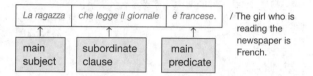

| La ragazza | che legge il giornale | è francese. |

main subject / subordinate clause / main predicate

/ The girl who is reading the newspaper is French.

There are two main types of subordinate or dependent clauses:

Relative Clause

A *relative clause* is a dependent clause introduced by a relative pronoun. (see §7.4).

Main sentence
La ragazza è italiana. / The girl is Italian.

Relative clause
(la ragazza) legge il giornale / The girl is reading the newspaper.

Relative pronoun (= che)
La ragazza che legge il giornale è italiana. / The girl who is reading the newspaper is Italian.

Temporal Clause

A *temporal* clause is a dependent clause introduced by subordinating conjunctions that involves time relations. A *conjunction* is a word that connects words, phrases, and clauses.

quando / when
se / if
dopo che / after
appena / as soon as
mentre / while

Examples

Quando Giacomo arriva, andremo al negozio. / When Jack arrives, we will go to the store.
Se viene Maria, vengo anch'io. / If Mary comes, I'll come too.
Dopo che sei andato via, è arrivata Sandra. / After you left, Sandra arrived.
La famiglia è arrivata appena sei andato via. / The family arrived as soon as you left.
Mentre tu dormivi, io leggevo il giornale. / While you were sleeping, I read the newspaper.

Other kinds of conjunctions can also introduce clauses into sentences. A number of these require the *subjunctive* form of the verb, and thus will be discussed in the sections dealing with the subjunctive (see §8.5).

Benché piova, esco lo stesso. / Although it is raining, I'm going out just the same.

To join two sentences, two clauses, two words, etc. simply use the conjunctions *e* (and) or *o* (or).

Examples

Maria studia e suo fratello guarda la TV. / Mary is studying and her brother is watching TV.

*La ragazza che ha i capelli biondi e che parla italiano molto bene
è americana.* / The girl with the blonde hair and who speaks
Italian quite well is American.
Gino e Gina parlano italiano. / Gino and Gina speak Italian.
Vengo con la macchina o a piedi. / I'm coming with the car or on
foot.

§2.4 INCOMPLETE SENTENCES

When we speak, we don't always use complete sentences,
that is, sentences with a stated subject and predicate.
Parts of a sentence may be left out when they are clearly
implied.

Examples

Come stai? / How are you?
Sto bene, grazie. / I am well, thanks.
Bene, grazie. / Well, thanks.

Quando è arrivato tuo padre? / When did your father arrive?
Mio padre è arrivato alle tre. / My father arrived at three o'clock.
È arrivato alle tre. / He arrived at three o'clock.

Quando sei andato al teatro? / When did you go to the theater?
Sono andato al teatro ieri. / I went to the theater yesterday.
Ieri. / Yesterday.

§2.5 ACTIVE VERSUS PASSIVE SENTENCES

*Il periodo attivo versus
il periodo passivo*

All the sentences illustrated so far have been *active* sentences. The verb in such sentences expresses the action performed by the subject. But for many active sentences there
are corresponding *passive* ones in which the action is performed *on* the subject.

Active

Maria legge il libro. / Mary reads the book.

Passive

Il libro è letto da Maria. / The book is read by Mary.

You will learn how to change active sentences into passive ones in Section §8.8.

§2.6 DIRECT AND INDIRECT SENTENCES

Il discorso diretto e indiretto

Sentences can be subdivided into two general categories: those conveying something directly and those conveying something indirectly. In general, *direct* speech involves talking directly to someone. *Indirect* speech involves talking about someone or something. Notice that there are differences between the two forms of speech.

Indirect speech

Carlo dice che i ragazzi sono italiani. / Carlo says that the boys are Italian.

Direct speech

Carlo chiede, "Ragazzi, siete italiani?" / Carlo asks, "Boys, are you Italian?"

Parts of Speech

§3.
Nouns

§3.1 WHAT ARE NOUNS?

> *Il nome/Il sostantivo*

Nouns are words that allow us to name and label the persons, objects, places, concepts, etc. that make up our world. In Italian, a noun generally can be recognized by its vowel ending, which indicates its gender (see §3.2) and number (see §3.3).

Examples

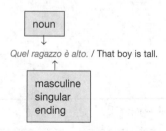

noun
↓
Quel ragazzo è alto. / That boy is tall.
↑
masculine singular ending

Quelle ragazze sono alte. / Those girls are tall.

Proper nouns are the names given to people and places. They are always capitalized.

Examples

Il signor Rossi è simpatico. / Mr. Rossi is pleasant.

Maria è felice. / Mary is happy.

L'Italia è bella. / Italy is beautiful.

Common nouns are all the other kinds of nouns used in a language. These can be "count" or "noncount."

Count nouns refer to persons, things, etc. that can be counted. They have both a singular and plural form.

Examples

Singular	**Plural**
la penna / the pen	*le penne* / the pens
il libro / the book	*i libri* / the books

Noncount nouns refer to persons, things, etc. that cannot be counted, and therefore normally have only a singular form.

Examples

l'acqua / water
lo zucchero / sugar
il pane / bread

Some noncount nouns can, of course, be used in a figurative way. In such cases they behave exactly like count nouns.

Example

le acque del mare / the waters of the sea

Common nouns are not capitalized unless they occur at the beginning of a sentence. Nouns referring to languages, speakers of a language, or inhabitants of an area normally are not capitalized.

Examples

L'italiano è una bella lingua. / Italian is a beautiful language.
Ci sono tanti spagnoli in quella città. / There are lots of Spaniards in that city.

However, there is a tendency now to imitate the English practice of capitalizing such nouns.

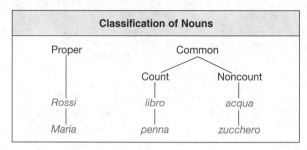

Classification of Nouns		
Proper	Common	
	Count	Noncount
Rossi	*libro*	*acqua*
Maria	*penna*	*zucchero*

§3.2 GENDER

> *Il genere*
> *maschile* = masculine
> *femminile* = feminine

Italian nouns have two genders: masculine and feminine. More will be said about genders in the next section (see §3.2–1). For now, it is important to know that this system of classification determines the form of both the articles (see Chapter 4) and adjectives (see Chapter 6) that accompany nouns in speech.

The ending of a noun gives us an important clue as to its gender.

> **Tip**
>
> Nouns ending with the vowel *-o* are normally masculine.

Examples

il ragazzo / the boy
il giorno / the day
l'aeroporto / the airport
Carlo / Charles
Belgio / Belgium

Nouns ending with the vowel *-a* are normally feminine.

Examples

la ragazza / the girl
la carta / paper
la valigia / the suitcase
Carla / Carla
l'Italia / Italy

Tip Nouns ending with the vowel *-o* are either masculine or feminine. To be sure about the gender of a specific noun ending in *-o*, you will have to consult a dictionary.

Examples

Masculine	**Feminine**
il dottore / the doctor	*la gente* / people
il padre / the father	*la madre* / the mother
il nome / the name	*la televisione* / television
Giuseppe / Joseph	*la notte* / night

Tip You can often identify the gender of a common noun by the form of its modifiers. Articles and adjectives in particular can help you determine if the noun is masculine or feminine.

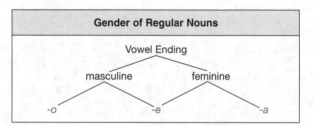

il giornale italiano / the Italian newspaper

The adjective form *italiano* gives away the gender of *giornale* and so does the article form *il*.

la notte lunga / the long night

The adjective form *lunga* gives away the gender of *notte* and so does the article form *la*.

Gender of Regular Nouns

Vowel Ending

masculine   feminine

-o   -e   -a

---

§3.2–1 Some Gender Patterns

The assigning of gender to nouns, especially those referring to an object or concept, is arbitrary. It is not possible, on the basis of the noun's meaning, to determine whether it will have a masculine or feminine ending. Noun endings, however, do reflect biological gender (i.e., sex). In general, male beings are designated by nouns ending in *-o* or *-e* (masculine endings) and female beings are designated by nouns ending in *-a* or *-e* (feminine endings).

Examples

Masculine

-o

il ragazzo / boy
lo zio / uncle

Feminine

-a

la ragazza / girl
la zia / aunt

il figlio / son
il gatto / cat (male)
l'americano / American (male)
Carlo / Charles
Paolo / Paul

la figlia / daughter
la gatta / cat (female)
l'americana / American (female)
Carla / Carla
Paola / Paula

il francese / French man
l'inglese / English man
il cantante / singer (male)
il nipote / nephew

la francese / French woman
l'inglese / English woman
la cantante / singer (female)
la nipote / niece

l'infermiere / nurse (male)
il cameriere / waiter

l'infermiera / nurse (female)
la cameriera / waitress

Exceptions

Il soprano (soprano) is a masculine noun referring to a female person.

La spia (spy) is a feminine noun and can refer to a male person.

In general, the names of trees are masculine, whereas the fruit they bear is feminine.

Examples

Masculine
il melo / apple tree
l'arancio / orange tree
il pesco / peach tree
il pero / pear tree
il ciliegio / cherry tree

Feminine
la mela / apple
l'arancia / orange
la pesca / peach
la pera / pear
la ciliegia / cherry

> **Exceptions**
>
> *Il limone* (lemon), *il fico* (fig), and *il mandarino* (mandarin) refer to both the tree and the fruit.

Masculine nouns ending in *-tore*, referring to male persons, often have corresponding feminine nouns ending in *-trice*, referring to female persons.

Masculine	Feminine	Translation
il fornitore	*la fornitrice*	supplier
il pittore	*la pittrice*	painter
l'autore	*l'autrice*	author
l'attore	*l'attrice*	actor
lo scultore	*la scultrice*	sculptor

Some masculine nouns referring to male beings have corresponding feminine nouns ending in *-essa* referring to female beings.

Masculine	Feminine	Translation
il dottore	*la dottoressa*	doctor
il professore	*la professoressa*	professor
l'avvocato	*l'avvocatessa*	lawyer
l'elefante	*l'elefantessa*	elephant

Some of the feminine forms above are, however, being eliminated, especially if they refer to professional people:

l'avvocato / male or female lawyer
lo scultore / male or female sculptor

§3.2–2 Nouns Ending in -*ista*

These nouns generally refer to professional persons. They can be either masculine (even if they end in -*a*) or feminine, according to whether they designate a male or female person.

Masculine	Feminine	Translation
il dentista	*la dentista*	dentist
il pianista	*la pianista*	pianist
il farmacista	*la farmacista*	pharmacist
il violinista	*la violinista*	violinist

§3.2–3 Nouns Ending in an Accented Vowel

A few Italian nouns end in an accented vowel. In general, those ending in -*à* and -*ù* are feminine; those ending in other accented vowels are masculine.

Examples

Masculine	Feminine
il tè / tea	*la città* / city
il caffè / coffee	*l'università* / university
il tassì / taxi	*la gioventù* / youth
il lunedì / Monday	*la virtù* / virtue

Exceptions

There are several exceptions to this pattern, notably: *il papà* (dad), *il pascià* ("the Pasha," a title of rank or honor placed after the name in the Ottoman Empire), and *il gagà* (the fop).

§3.2–4 Borrowed Nouns

These are nouns that have been borrowed from other languages, primarily English. Unless they refer to a female being, they are all treated as masculine nouns.

Examples

lo sport / sport
il tram / streetcar, trolley
il computer / computer
il clacson / car horn
il tennis / tennis
l'autobus / bus

§3.2–5 Nouns Ending in *-ema* and *-amma*

These nouns correspond to English nouns ending in *-em* and *-am*, and are of Greek origin. They all are masculine, even if they end in *-a*.

Examples

il problema / the problem
il teorema / the theorem
il programma / the program
il telegramma / the telegram
il diagramma / the diagram

§3.2–6 Nouns Ending in *-si*

These nouns correspond to English nouns ending in *-sis*, and also are of Greek origin. They all are feminine.

la crisi / the crisis
la tesi / the thesis
l'analisi / the analysis
l'ipotesi / the hypothesis

Exception

Il brindisi ([drinking] toast) is masculine; it is of Germanic origin.

§3.3 NUMBER

Il numero
singolare = singular
plurale = plural

Number means that a word can be *singular* (= referring to one person, thing, etc.) or *plural* (= referring to more than one). Recall that noncount nouns (see §3.1) have only a singular form.

Examples

l'acqua / water
il pane / bread
la fame / hunger
la sete / thirst
il pepe / pepper
il sale / salt

A few nouns occur only in the plural form. They refer to things made up of more than one part.

Examples

le forbici / scissors
gli occhiali / (eye)glasses
i pantaloni / pants
le mutande / underwear
i baffi / mustache

§3.3–1   Plural of Regular Nouns

Common count nouns have both a singular and plural form. Regular Italian nouns (see §3.2) are put into the plural by making the following changes to the vowel endings.

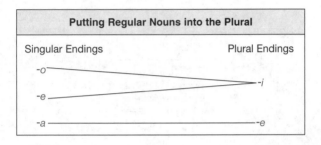

Putting Regular Nouns into the Plural

Singular Endings   Plural Endings

-o
                                                     -i
-e

-a   -e

Examples

Singular

-o

il ragazzo / the boy
il giorno / the day
l'aeroporto / the airport

-e

il padre / the father
il cameriere / the waiter
la madre / the mother
la notte / the night
l'attore / the actor

-a

la ragazza / the girl
la mela / the apple
la gonna / the skirt

Plural

-i

i ragazzi / the boys
i giorni / the days
gli aeroporti / the airports

-i

i padri / the fathers
i camerieri / the waiters
le madri / the mothers
le notti / the nights
gli attori / the actors

-e

le ragazze / the girls
le mele / the apples
le gonne / the skirts

Be careful! The noun *gente* (people) is singular in Italian.

> *La gente parla troppo.* / People speak too much.

Note that the plural ending -*i* is used when the noun refers to both male *and* female beings taken together as a group.

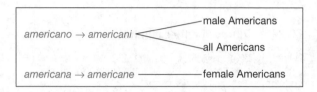

americano → americani ──── male Americans

americano → americani ──── all Americans

americana → americane ──── female Americans

§3.3–2   Plural of Nouns Ending in -*ista*, -*ema*, and -*amma*

Nouns ending in -*ista* are either masculine or feminine (see §3.2–2). The plural of such nouns is obtained as follows:

> If the noun refers to male persons, then its plural is -*isti*; if it refers to female persons, then its plural form is -*iste*

Examples

Singular	Plural
il dentista / the (male) dentist	*i dentisti* / the (male) dentists
la dentista / the (female) dentist	*le dentiste* / the (female) dentists
il turista / the (male) tourist	*i turisti* / the (male) tourists
la turista / the (female) tourist	*le turiste* / the (female) tourists

Note that in this case as well, the plural ending -*i* is used to designate both male and female beings.

> *i turisti* / male tourists *or* all tourists
> *le turiste* / female tourists.

All nouns ending in -*ema* and -*amma* are masculine (see §3.2–5). To pluralize such nouns change the endings to -*emi* and -*ammi*.

Examples

Singular	Plural
il problema / the problem	*i problemi* / the problems
il programma / the program	*i programmi* / the programs
il diagramma / the diagram	*i diagrammi* / the diagrams

§3.3–3 Plural of Other Nouns

Nouns ending in -*si* (see §3.2–6) and in an accented vowel (see §3.2–3), as well as borrowed nouns (see §3.2–4), do not undergo any changes in the plural.

Examples

Singular	Plural
la crisi / the crisis	*le crisi* / the crises
la città / the city	*le città* / the cities
il computer / the computer	*i computer* / the computers

§3.3–4 Spelling Peculiarities

When putting nouns that end in -*co*, -*go*, -*ca*, -*ga*, -*cio*, -*gio*, -*cia*, -*gia*, and -*io* into the plural, follow the patterns given below.

Nouns ending in -*co*

Change the -*co* to -*chi* when -*a*, -*o*, -*u*, or a consonant precedes it; change it to -*ci* when -*e* or -*i* precedes it.

The -*chi* represents a "hard" *k* sound, the -*ci* a "soft" sound.

Examples

Singular

baco / silkworm
fuoco / fire
buco / hole
parco / park
tedesco / German

Plural

bachi / silkworms
fuochi / fires
buchi / holes
parchi / parks
tedeschi / Germans

greco / Greek
amico / friend
medico / (medical) doctor

greci / Greeks
amici / friends
medici / (medical) doctors

Exceptions

porco (pig) → *porci*
fico (fig) → *fichi*

Nouns ending in *-go*

Change to *-ghi* in most cases. However, when the noun ends in the suffix *-logo* and refers to a profession, career, or activity, then the appropriate plural suffix is *-logi*.

The *-ghi* represents a hard sound, the *-gi* a soft sound.

Examples

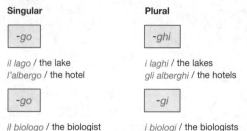

Singular	Plural
il lago / the lake	*i laghi* / the lakes
l'albergo / the hotel	*gli alberghi* / the hotels
il biologo / the biologist	*i biologi* / the biologists
lo psicologo / the psychologist	*gli psicologi* / the psychologists

But be careful! Not all nouns ending in *-logo* refer to the same kinds of things. In such cases, the *-go* is changed to *-ghi* in the plural.

Examples

Singular	**Plural**
il catalogo / the catalog	*i cataloghi* / the catalogs
il dialogo / the dialogue	*i dialoghi* / the dialogues

The above rules are to be considered only as guidelines.

Nouns ending in *-ca* and *-ga*

These are always pluralized with the hard sounds *-che* and *-ghe*, respectively.

Examples

Singular	**Plural**
amica / (female) friend	*amiche* / (female) friends
paga / pay (check)	*paghe* / pay (checks)

Nouns ending in *-cio*, *-gio*, *-cia*, *-gia*, and *-io*

If the *i* is stressed in the singular, then it is retained in the plural. If the *i* is not pronounced (as in English *social* and *Belgium*), it is not kept in the plural. In masculine nouns, this means that only one *i* is used.

Examples

Singular	Plural
farmacia (stressed) / pharmacy	*farmacie* / pharmacies
bugia (stressed) / lie	*bugie* / lies
bacio / kiss	*baci* / kisses
orologio / watch/clock	*orologi* / watches/clocks
arancia / orange (fruit)	*arance* / oranges
valigia / suitcase	*valige* / suitcases
zio (stressed) / uncle	*zii* / uncles
figlio / son	*figli* / sons

Exception

Camicia (shirt) is pluralized as *camicie* even though the *-i* in the ending *-cia* is not stressed.

Tip

If you have difficulty remembering that *ch* represents a "hard" *k* sound, just try to think of English words that use *ch* in the same way.

chemistry   *ache*   *charisma*

§3.3–5 Neuter Plurals

Like the English nouns "memorandum" and "compendium," which are pluralized by replacing the -*um* with -*a* ("memoranda" and "compendia"), Italian also has a few nouns whose plural forms end in -*a*. These derive Latin neuter forms that were pluralized in this way.

> Notice that in Italian, Latin neuter nouns are masculine in the singular but feminine in the plural!

Examples

Singular	Plural
il dito / the finger	*le dita* / the fingers
il labbro / the lip	*le labbra* / the lips
il paio / the pair	*le paia* / the pairs
il miglio / the mile	*le miglia* / the miles

There are not too many of these nouns, and most refer to parts of the human body.

§3.3–6 Miscellaneous Irregularities

Some nouns are abbreviations, and therefore do not change in the plural:

Examples

Singular	Plural
l'auto / the car	*le auto* / the cars
(from: *l'automobile*)	(*le automobili*)
il cinema / the movies	*i cinema* / the movie theaters
(from: *il cinematografo*)	(*i cinematografi*)
la foto / the photo	*le foto* / the photos
(from: *la fotografia*)	(*le fotografie*)

Some common nouns that are completely irregular are:

Examples

Singular	**Plural**
la mano / the hand (f.)	*le mani* / the hands
l'uomo / the man (m.)	*gli uomini* / the men
la radio / the radio (f.)	*le radio* / the radios

§3.4 TITLES

I titoli

The final -*e* of a masculine title is dropped before a name. This rule does not apply to feminine titles.

Examples

Masculine Title	**Used Before a Name**
il signore / the gentleman	*il signor Rossi* / Mr. Rossi
il professore / the professor	*il professor Verdi* / Professor Verdi
il dottore / the doctor	*il dottor Bianchi* / Dr. Bianchi
l'avvocato / the lawyer	*l'avvocato Tozzi* / the lawyer Tozzi

Feminine Title	**Used Before a Name**
la signora / the lady	*la signora Rossi* / Mrs. Rossi
la professoressa / the professor	*la professoressa Verdi* / Professor Verdi
la dottoressa / the doctor	*la dottoressa Bianchi* / Dr. Bianchi

§3.5 NOUN SUFFIXES

I suffissi

In some cases, you can change the meaning of a noun by adding a suffix such as the following:

-*ino*/-*ina* to add the nuance of "little" or "small" to the noun.

Examples

il ragazzo	*il ragazzino* / the little boy
la ragazza	*la ragazzina* / the little girl

-one/*-ona* to add the nuance of "big" or "large" to the noun.

Examples

il ragazzo	*il ragazzone* / the big boy
la ragazza	*la ragazzona* / the big girl

-accio/*-accia* to add the nuance of "bad" to the noun.

Examples

il ragazzo	*il ragazzaccio* / the bad boy
la ragazza	*la ragazzaccia* / the bad girl

Tip	Be very careful when using these suffixes! They have many shades of meaning and can be used incorrectly. To avoid offending anyone, be absolutely sure of the meaning.

§3.6 COMPOUND NOUNS

Le parole composte

Compound nouns are made up of two parts of speech:

Compound Noun

hand	kerchief
↑	↑
noun +	noun

To form the plural of such nouns in Italian, observe the following guidelines:

Most compound nouns are pluralized in the normal fashion (see §3.3–1).

Singular
l'arcobaleno / rainbow
la ferrovia / railroad

Plural
gli arcobaleni / rainbows
le ferrovie / railroads

In some cases, both parts of the compound noun are pluralized.

Singular
la cassaforte / (money) safe

Plural
le casseforti / safes

Other compound nouns, especially those that are made up of a verb, do not change.

Singular
il cacciavite / screwdriver
il salvagente / life jacket

Plural
i cacciavite / screwdrivers
i salvagente / life jackets

As you can see, pluralizing compound nouns can be a complicated task. Like most Italians do, you would be wise to check a dictionary to be sure you have pluralized a compound noun correctly.

§4.
Articles

§4.1 WHAT ARE ARTICLES?

> *Gli articoli*

Articles are words used to signal nouns and to specify their application.

Specific	**Nonspecific**
il libro / the book	*un libro* / a book

The article that allows one to signal persons, objects, etc., in a specific way is called *definite*. The article that allows one to designate nonspecific persons, objects, etc. is called *indefinite*.

Demonstratives will be included in this chapter, even though you will probably find them listed as adjectives in most grammars. They are included here because they too have the function of specifying a noun in some way. More precisely, demonstratives allow us to specify whether someone or something is relatively near or far.

Near	**Far**
questo libro / this book	*quel libro* / that book

§4.2 FORMS

Definite and indefinite articles, as well as demonstratives, vary according to the noun's gender, number, and initial sound.

Tip

It may help to remember that the English indefinite article also varies according to the initial sound of the following noun or adjective.

Before a consonant
a boy
a friend

Before a vowel
an egg
an angel

§4.2–1 The Definite Article

L'articolo determinativo

The forms of the definite article are:

BEFORE MASCULINE NOUNS	Singular	Plural
Beginning with *z*, or *s* + consonant	*lo*	*gli*
Beginning with any vowel	*l'*	*gli*
Beginning with any other consonant	*il* ——— *i*	
BEFORE FEMININE NOUNS		
Beginning with any consonant	*la*	*le*
Beginning with any vowel	*l'*	*le*

Examples

Singular	**Plural**

lo zio / the uncle	*gli zii* / the uncles
lo zero / the zero	*gli zeri* / the zeroes
lo studente / the student	*gli studenti* / the students
lo specchio / the mirror	*gli specchi* / the mirrors
lo sbaglio / the mistake	*gli sbagli* / the mistakes

l'amico / the friend	*gli amici* / the friends
l'italiano / the Italian	*gli italiani* / the Italians
l'orologio / the watch	*gli orologi* / the watches

il padre / the father	*i padri* / the fathers
il fratello / the brother	*i fratelli* / the brothers
il nonno / the grandfather	*i nonni* / the grandfathers

la madre / the mother	*le madri* / the mothers
la sorella / the sister	*le sorelle* / the sisters
la nonna / the grandmother	*le nonne* / the grandmothers

l'amica / the (female) friend	*le amiche* / the (female) friends
l'entrata / the entrance	*le entrate* / the entrances
l'uscita / the exit	*le uscite* / the exits

Be careful! With feminine nouns beginning with *z*, or *s* + consonant, you use *la: la zia* (the aunt), *la scuola* (the school).

The masculine form *lo* (plural *gli*) is also used in front of nouns beginning with *ps* or *gn* (and a few other unusual initial sounds).

Examples

lo psicologo / the psychologist	*gli psicologi* / the psychologists
lo gnocco / the dumpling	*gli gnocchi* / the dumplings

Be careful! When an adjective precedes the noun, you will have to adjust the definite article according to its beginning sound.

la zia / the aunt	*la vecchia zia* / the old aunt
lo studente / the student	*l'altro studente* / the other student
gli amici / the friends	*i vecchi amici* / the old friends
l'orologio / the watch	*il bell'orologio* / the nice watch

Tip

It may help to remember that a similar pattern applies in English.

a boy	*an* intelligent boy
an apple	*a* good apple

§4.2–2 The Indefinite Article

*L'articolo
indeterminativo*

The forms of the indefinite article in the singular are as follows. Pluralization of the indefinite article is discussed in Chapter 5.

BEFORE MASCULINE NOUNS	
Beginning with *z* or *s* + consonant ———————— *uno*	
Beginning with any other sound ———————— *un* (consonant or vowel)	
BEFORE FEMININE NOUNS	
Beginning with any consonant ———————— *una*	
Beginning with any vowel ———————— *un'*	

Note that the apostrophe (*un'*) is used only when the indefinite article is in front of a feminine noun beginning with a vowel.

As in the case of the definite article form *lo* (see §4.2–1), the indefinite form *uno* is also used in front of nouns beginning with *ps* and *gn*.

Examples

uno	*un*
uno zio / an uncle	*un piede* / a foot
uno sbaglio / a mistake	*un braccio* / an arm
uno psicologo / a psychologist	*un occhio* / an eye
uno gnocco / a dumpling	*un orecchio* / an ear

una	*un'*
una zia / an aunt	*un'unghia* / a fingernail
una bocca / a mouth	*un'automobile* / an automobile
una gamba / a leg	*un'ora* / an hour

Don't forget! When an adjective precedes the noun, you will have to adjust the indefinite article according to the beginning sound.

uno zio / an uncle *un caro zio* / a dear uncle
un'amica / a friend *una cara amica* / a dear friend

§4.2–3 The Demonstratives

I dimostrativi

The demonstrative forms are:

DEMONSTRATIVE INDICATING "NEARNESS"	
Before Masculine Nouns	
Singular	**Plural**
questo	*questi*
Before Feminine Nouns	
Singular	**Plural**
questa	*queste*

Examples

questo

questo sbaglio / this mistake
questo giornale / this newspaper
questo esercizio / this exercise

questi

questi sbagli / these mistakes
questi giornali / these newspapers
questi esercizi / these exercises

questa	queste

questa stanza / this room
questa ora / this hour

queste stanze / these rooms
queste ore / these hours

The form *quest'* is often used before singular nouns (or modifying adjectives) beginning with a vowel.

questo esercizio or *quest'esercizio* / this exercise
questa ora or *quest'ora* / this hour
questa ultima giornata or *quest'ultima giornata* / this last day
questo incredibile giorno or *quest'incredibile giorno* / this incredible day

DEMONSTRATIVE INDICATING "FARNESS"		
Before Masculine Nouns		
	Singular	**Plural**
Beginning with *z* or *s* + consonant	*quello*	*quegli*
Beginning with any vowel	*quell'*	
Beginning with any other consonant	*quel*	*quei*
Before Feminine Nouns		
Beginning with any consonant	*quella*	*quelle*
Beginning with any vowel	*quell'*	

As with the article forms *lo* and *uno* (see §4.2–1 and §4.2.–2), the form *quello* (plural *quegli*) is also used before those few nouns beginning with *ps* and *gn*.

Examples

quello	quegli

quello zingaro / that gypsy
quello spagnolo / that Spaniard
quello psicologo / that psychologist
quello gnocco / that dumpling

quegli zingari / those gypsies
quegli spagnoli / those Spaniards
quegli psicologi / those psychologists
quegli gnocchi / those dumplings

quell'	quegli

quell'albero / that tree
quell'esame / that exam

quegli alberi / those trees
quegli esami / those exams

quel	quei

quel dottore / that doctor
quel tavolo / that table

quei dottori / those doctors
quei tavoli / those tables

quella	quelle

quella porta / that door
quella finestra / that window

quelle porte / those doors
quelle finestre / those windows

quell'	quelle

quell'entrata / that entrance
quell'uscita / that exit

quelle entrate / those entrances
quelle uscite / those exits

> Be careful! As with articles, when an adjective precedes a noun, you will have to change the demonstrative according to the adjective's initial sound.

quello zingaro / that gypsy
quella porta / that door
quegli amici / those friends

quel simpatico zingaro / that nice gypsy
quell'ultima porta / that last door
quei simpatici amici / those nice friends

Tip

> If you look very closely, you will see that this
> demonstrative behaves exactly like the definite
> article.
>
> | quello zio | = | lo zio |
> |--------------|---|-----------|
> | quell'amico | = | l'amico |
> | quei ragazzi | = | i ragazzi |
>
> etc.

§4.3   USES

Note the following differences between English and Italian
uses of articles and demonstratives.

> The definite article is used in front of noncount nouns
> (see §3.1) used as subjects (normally at the start of a
> sentence).

Examples

L'acqua è un liquido. / Water is a liquid.
Il cibo è necessario per vivere. / Food is necessary to live.
La pazienza è una virtù. / Patience is a virtue.

> The definite article is also used with count nouns in the
> plural to express generalizations.

Examples

Gli italiani sono simpatici. / Italians are nice.
I libri ci aiutano a capire. / Books help us understand.

As a guideline, just remember that you *cannot* start an Italian
sentence with a common noun without its article.

The definite article is used in front of geographical names (continents, countries, states, rivers, islands, mountains, etc.), except cities.

Examples

l'Italia / Italy
la Sicilia / Sicily
gli Stati Uniti / the United States
il Tevere / the Tiber
la California / California
il Mediterraneo / the Mediterranean
il Belgio / Belgium
le Alpi / the Alps
il Piemonte / Piedmont

But:

Roma / Rome
Berlino / Berlin
Parigi / Paris

The definite article is usually dropped after the preposition *in* and before an unmodified geographical noun.

Examples

Vado in Italia. / I'm going to Italy.
Abito in Francia. / I live in France.

But when the noun is modified:

Vado nell'Italia centrale. / I'm going to central Italy.
Abito nella Francia meridionale. / I live in southern France.

The definite article is used with dates.

Examples

Il 1492 è un anno importante. / 1492 is an important year.
Oggi è il tre novembre. / Today is November third.

The definite article is commonly used in place of possessive adjectives (see §6.4–3) when referring to family members (singular only), parts of the body, and clothing.

Examples

Oggi vado in centro con la zia. / Today I'm going downtown with my aunt.
Mi fa male la gamba. / My leg hurts.
Mario non si mette mai la giacca. / Mario never puts his jacket on.

The definite article is used with the days of the week to indicate an habitual action.

Examples

Il lunedì gioco a tennis. / On Mondays I play tennis.
La domenica vado in chiesa. / On Sundays I go to church.

Note that the days of the week, except Sunday, are masculine. The definite article is not used when a specific day is intended.

Il lunedì di solito gioco a tennis, ma lunedì vado via. / On Mondays I usually play tennis, but (this) Monday I'm going away.

The definite article is used with titles, unless you are speaking directly to the person mentioned.

Examples

Speaking about
Il dottor Verdi è italiano. /
Dr. Verdi is Italian.

Speaking to
Buon giorno, dottor Verdi. /
Hello, Dr. Verdi.

La professoressa Bianchi è molto intelligente. /
Professor Bianchi is very intelligent.

Professoressa Bianchi, dove abita? /
Professor Bianchi, where do you live?

The definite article is used before the names of languages and nouns referring to school subjects.

Examples

Impariamo lo spagnolo. / We are learning Spanish.
Studio la matematica. / I am studying mathematics.

The definite article is dropped after the prepositions *di* and *in*.

Examples

Ecco il libro di spagnolo. / Here is the Spanish book.
Sono bravo in matematica. / I'm good in math.

The definite article is used with *scorso* (last) and *prossimo* (next) in time expressions.

Examples

la settimana scorsa / last week
il mese prossimo / next month

Note that the definite article is not used in some common expressions.

a destra / to the right
a sinistra / to the left
a casa / at home

The indefinite article also means "one."

> *un'arancia* / an orange *or* one orange
> *un libro* / a book *or* one book
> *una penna* / a pen *or* one pen

The indefinite article is not used in exclamations starting with *Che . . . !*

Examples

> *Che film!* / What a film!
> *Che bel vestito!* / What a beautiful dress!

Finally, remember to repeat the articles and demonstratives before every noun.

Examples

> *un ragazzo e una ragazza* / a boy and girl
> *il ragazzo e la ragazza* / the boy and girl
> *questo ragazzo e questa ragazza* / this boy and girl
> *quel ragazzo e quella ragazza* / that boy and girl

§5.
Partitives

§5.1 WHAT ARE PARTITIVES?

I partitivi

Partitives are structures placed before nouns that indicate a part of something as distinct from its whole.

dell'acqua / some water
degli esami / some exams

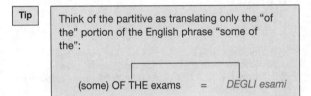

Tip	Think of the partitive as translating only the "of the" portion of the English phrase "some of the":

(some) OF THE exams   =   *DEGLI esami*

§5.2 WITH COUNT NOUNS

Before count nouns (see §3.1), the partitive can be considered to be the plural of the indefinite article (see §4.2–2). The most commonly used type of partitive in this case consists of the preposition *di* + the appropriate plural forms of the definite article.

Masculine Forms
di + i = dei   *di + i libri = dei libri* / some books
di + gli = degli   *di + gli specchi = degli specchi* / some mirrors

Feminine Form
di + le = delle   *di + le penne = delle penne* / some pens

Examples

uno / un	degli

uno sbaglio / a mistake
un albero / a tree

degli sbagli / some mistakes
degli alberi / some trees

un	dei

un bicchiere / a glass
un coltello / a knife

dei bicchieri / some glasses
dei coltelli / some knives

una / un'	delle

una forchetta / a fork
una sedia / a chair
un'automobile /
   an automobile

delle forchette / some forks
delle sedie / some chairs
delle automobili / some automobiles

In place of these forms, the pronouns *alcuni* (m.) and *alcune* (f.) can be used to express the idea of "some" or, more precisely, "several." They are used only in the plural.

Examples

degli zii / some uncles
dei bicchieri /
   some glasses
delle forchette /
   some forks
delle amiche /
   some friends (f.)

alcuni zii / several (a few) uncles
alcuni bicchieri / several
   (a few) glasses
alcune forchette / several
   (a few) forks
alcune amiche / several (a few)
   friends (f.)

Actually, these two types can be used together in expressions such as:

some	of the	books
|	|	|
alcuni	*dei*	*libri*

some	of the	mirrors
|	|	|
alcuni	*degli*	*specchi*

some	of the	pens
|	|	|
alcune	*delle*	*penne*

The invariable pronoun *qualche* can also be used to express partiality. But be careful with this one! It must be followed by a *singular* noun, even though the meaning is plural!

some	books		some	pens
|	|		|	|
qualche	*libro* (sing.)		*qualche*	*penna* (sing.)

Tip

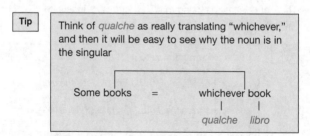

Think of *qualche* as really translating "whichever," and then it will be easy to see why the noun is in the singular

Some books = whichever book
\| \|
qualche   *libro*

The pronoun forms (*qualche* or *alcuni/alcune*) are often used at the start of sentences, rather than the *degli/dei/delle* forms. Once again, be careful with *qualche*: It requires a singular verb!

Examples

Alcuni studenti studiano il francese. / Some students study
French.
Qualche studente studia il francese. / Some students study
French.

In colloquial Italian, it is not unusual to find that the partitive is
omitted (when the noun is not the first word in a sentence).

Examples

Voglio della carne. = *Voglio carne.* / I want (some) meat.
Mangio degli spaghetti. = *Mangio spaghetti.* / I'm eating (some)
spaghetti.

In negative sentences, the partitive is omitted.

Examples

Affirmative Sentence	**Negative Sentence**
Ho dei biglietti. / I have some tickets.	*Non ho biglietti.* / I don't have any tickets.
Voglio delle paste. / I want some pastries.	*Non voglio paste.* / I don't want any pastries.

The negative partitive can be rendered by *non . . . nessuno.*
Think of *nessuno* as being made up of *ness* + indefinite
article.

Tip	*nessuno* corresponds to *uno: uno studente/ nessuno studente* *nessun* corresponds to *un: un biglietto/nessun biglietto* *nessuna* corresponds to *una: una signora/nessuna signora* *nessun'* corresponds to *un': un'automobile/ nessun'automobile*

This means that the noun is always in the singular, even
though the meaning is plural.

Examples

Affirmative Sentence	**Negative Sentence**
Carlo compra degli specchi. / Charles buys some mirrors.	*Carlo non compra nessuno specchio.* / Charles does not buy any mirrors.
Carla compra delle caramelle. / Carla buys some candies.	*Carla non compra nessuna caramella.* / Carla does not buy any candies.

§5.3   WITH NONCOUNT NOUNS

With noncount nouns (see §3.1), the partitive is rendered by either *di* + the singular forms of the definite article (according to the noun), or by the expression *un po' di* ("a bit of").

Masculine Forms

di + il = del   *di + il vino = del vino* / some wine
di + lo = dello   *di + lo zucchero = dello zucchero* / some sugar
di + l' = dell'   *di + l' orzo = dell'orzo* / some barley

Feminine Form

di + la = della   *di + la pasta = della pasta* / some pasta

Examples

Voglio del pane. = Voglio un po' di pane. / I want some bread.
Lui vuole dello zucchero. = Lui vuole un po' di zucchero. /
  He wants some sugar.
Maria mangia dell'insalata. = Maria mangia un po' di insalata. /
  Mary eats some salad.
*Preferisco mangiare della carne. = Preferisco mangiare
  un po' di carne.* / I prefer to eat some meat.

§5.4   SUMMARY

The following chart summarizes the various partitive forms:

WITH COUNT NOUNS	
Singular Forms of the Indefinite Article	Corresponding Partitive Forms
Masculine *un* *un libro* / a book	Masculine *dei, alcuni, qualche, nessun* *dei libri* / some books *alcuni libri* / several books *qualche libro* / some books *nessun libro* / no books
un *un amico* / a friend	*degli, alcuni, qualche, nessun* *degli amici* / some friends *alcuni amici* / several friends *qualche amico* / some friends *nessuno amico* / no friends
uno *uno studente* / a student	*degli, alcuni, qualche, nessuno* *degli studenti* / some students *alcuni studenti* / several students *qualche studente* / some students *nessun studente* / no students
Feminine *una* *una penna* / a pen	Feminine *delle, alcune, qualche, nessuna* *delle penne* / some pens *alcune penne* / several pens *qualche penna* / some pens *nessuna penna* / no pens
un' *un'amica* / a friend	*delle, alcune, qualche, nessun'* *delle amiche* / some friends *alcune amiche* / several friends *qualche amica* / some friends *nessun'amica* / no friends

WITH NONCOUNT NOUNS	
Masculine Forms *del*	Equivalent Forms
del riso / some rice	*un po' di riso*
dell'	
dell'orzo / some barley	*un po' di orzo*
dello	
dello zucchero / some sugar	*un po' di zucchero*
Feminine Forms *della*	
della carne / some meat	*un po' di carne*
dell'	
dell'acqua / some water	*un po' di acqua*

Remember! As in the case of articles and demonstratives (see Chapter 4), you may have to change the partitive forms when an adjective precedes the noun.

Examples

degli zii / some uncles   *dei simpatici zii* / some nice uncles
dell'acqua / some water   *della buon'acqua* / some good water

§6.
Adjectives

§6.1 WHAT ARE ADJECTIVES?

> *Gli aggettivi*

Adjectives are words that modify, or describe, nouns. They are placed before or after the noun they modify.

> *È una casa nuova.* / It's a new house.
>
> *È il mio libro.* / It's my book.

> **Tip**
>
> Adjectives can be easily recognized. They are generally distinguishable by predictable changes in the final vowel:
>
> *il libro nuovo* / the new book
> *i libri nuovi* / the new books
> *la rivista nuova* / the new magazine
> *le riviste nuove* / the new magazines

§6.2 AGREEMENT

> *L'accordo*

Adjectives must agree with the nouns they modify. This means that an adjective must correspond in gender and number with the noun. Thus, the ending of an adjective depends on whether the noun is masculine or feminine, singular or plural.

There are two types of adjectives according to their endings.

Adjectives that end in -*o* (masculine singular) have the following set of endings that agree with the noun:

	Singular	Plural
Masculine	-*o*	-*i*
Feminine	-*a*	-*e*

Examples

Singular	Plural
l'uomo alto / the tall man	*gli uomini alti* / the tall men
il figlio alto / the tall son	*i figli alti* / the tall sons
la donna alta / the tall woman	*le donne alte* / the tall women
la madre alta / the tall mother	*le madri alte* / the tall mothers

Adjectives that end in -*e* in the singular have two endings, according to whether they modify a singular noun (masculine or feminine) or plural noun (masculine or feminine):

	Singular	Plural
Masculine or Feminine	-*e*	-*i*

Examples

Singular	Plural
il medico intelligente / the intelligent doctor	*i medici intelligenti* / the intelligent doctors
il padre intelligente / the intelligent father	*i padri intelligenti* / the intelligent fathers
la donna intelligente / the intelligent woman	*le donne intelligenti* / the intelligent women
la madre intelligente / the intelligent mother	*le madri intelligenti* / the intelligent mothers

A few adjectives are invariable; that is, their ending never changes. The most common are the adjectives of color: *marrone* (brown), *arancione* (orange), *viola* (violet, purple), *rosa* (pink), and *blu* (dark blue).

Examples

Singular	Plural
il vestito marrone / the brown suit	*i vestiti marrone* / the brown suits
la giacca marrone / the brown jacket	*le giacche marrone* / the brown jackets
la matita arancione / the orange crayon	*le matite arancione* / the orange crayons
lo zaino viola / the purple backpack	*gli zaini viola* / the purple backpacks
l'abito rosa /the pink dress	*gli abiti rosa* /the pink dresses
la sciarpa blu / the dark blue scarf	*le sciarpe blu* / the dark blue scarves

When two nouns are modified, the adjective is always in the plural. If the two nouns are feminine, then the appropriate feminine plural form is used. If the two nouns are both masculine, or of mixed gender, then the appropriate masculine plural form is used.

Examples

Both Feminine

La maglia e la borsa sono rosse. / The sweater and the purse are red.

Both Masculine

Il cappotto e l'impermeabile sono rossi. / The coat and the raincoat are red.

Mixed Gender

La maglia e il cappotto sono rossi. / The sweater and the coat are red.

§6.3 POSITION

Interrogative (see §6.4–2) and possessive (see §6.4–3) adjectives *precede* the noun they modify, whereas descriptive adjectives (see §6.4–1) generally *follow* the noun.

> *Quante scarpe hai comprato?* / How many shoes did you buy?
> *quante* = interrogative adjective
>
> *I tuoi pantaloni sono lunghi.* / Your pants are long.
> *i tuoi* = possessive adjective
>
> *Ieri ho comprato una camicia bianca.* /
>   Yesterday I bought a white shirt.
> *bianca* = descriptive adjective

Some descriptive adjectives, however, can be used before or after the noun.

Examples

È una bella camicia.	or	*È una camicia bella.* / It's a beautiful shirt.
Maria è una ragazza simpatica.	or	*Maria è una simpatica ragazza.* / Mary is a nice girl.

You will eventually learn which descriptive adjectives can come before through practice and use. As you read something, make a note of the position of the adjective.

Be careful! As discussed in Chapter 4, you will have to change the form of the article, demonstrative, etc. when you put the adjective before a noun.

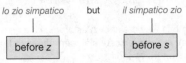

> *lo zio simpatico*   but   *il simpatico zio*

before *z*   before *s*

Some common descriptive adjectives that can come before or after a noun are:

bello / beautiful	*cattivo* / bad	*piccolo* / small, little
brutto / ugly	*giovane* / young	*povero* / poor
buono / good	*grande* / big, large	*simpatico* /
		nice, charming
caro / dear	*nuovo* / new	*vecchio* / old

But be careful! A few of these adjectives change meaning according to their position.

Examples

È un ragazzo povero. = He is a poor boy (not wealthy).
È un povero ragazzo. = He is a poor boy (deserving of pity).
È un amico vecchio. = He is an old friend (in age).
È un vecchio amico. = He is an old friend (for many years).

Tip

As always, when you are unsure of the meaning and use of an adjective, check a dictionary.

Descriptive adjectives can also be separated from the noun they modify by what is called a *linking* verb. The most common linking verbs are *essere* (to be), *sembrare* (to seem), and *diventare* (to become).

Examples

Quella casa è nuova. / That house is new.
Quell'uomo sembra giovane. / That man seems young.
Questa camicia sta diventando vecchia. / This shirt is becoming old.

Adjectives used in this way are known as *predicate adjectives* because they occur in the predicate slot, *after* the verb that links them to the noun they modify.

One final word about the position of descriptive adjectives! When these adjectives are accompanied by an adverb, another adjective, or some other part of speech, they must *follow* the noun.

Examples

È un simpatico ragazzo. / He is a pleasant boy.

BUT

È un ragazzo molto simpatico. / He is a very pleasant boy.
È un ragazzo simpatico e bravo. / He is a pleasant and good boy.

§6.4 TYPES

The four most common types of adjectives are *demonstrative, descriptive, interrogative,* and *possessive.* Demonstrative adjectives have already been discussed in §4.2–3.

§6.4–1 Descriptive

> *Gli aggettivi qualificativi*

Descriptive adjectives specify a quality of the noun they modify. They make up the largest group of adjectives. As already discussed (see §6.2), descriptive adjectives generally follow the noun.

Examples

È un esame difficile. / It's a difficult exam.
Porta una giacca blu. / He's wearing a dark blue jacket.
È una strada lunga. / It's a long road.

Of the adjectives that can come before the noun, *buono* (good), *bello* (beautiful), *santo* (saint[ly]), and *grande* (big, large) change in form when they are placed before.

Tip	The singular forms of *buono* undergo the same kind of changes as the indefinite article (see §4.2–2). *buon* corresponds to *un*: *un giorno / buon giorno* *buona* corresponds to *una*: *una giornata / buona giornata* etc.

BEFORE MASCULINE NOUNS		
	Singular	**Plural**
Beginning with *z*, *s* + consonant, *ps*, *gn*	*buono*	*buoni*
Beginning with any other sound (vowel or consonant)	*buon*	

BEFORE FEMININE NOUNS	
Beginning with any consonant	*buona*
Beginning with any vowel	*buon'*

(*buona*/*buon'* → *buone*)

When it is placed after the noun, *buono* is treated as a normal descriptive adjective ending in *-o* (see §6.2).

Examples

Singular

un buono zio or *uno zio buono* / a good uncle
un buon libro or *un libro buono* / a good book
un buon amico or *un amico buono* / a good friend
una buona macchina or *una macchina buona* / a good car
una buon'amica or *un'amica buona* / a good friend

Plural

dei buoni zii or *degli zii buoni* / some good uncles
dei buoni amici or *degli amici buoni* / some good friends
delle buone macchine or *delle macchine buone* / some good cars
delle buone amiche or *delle amiche buone* / some good friends

Notice that the apostrophe is used only with the feminine form (*buon'*), as is the case for the indefinite article (see §4.2–2).

> When referring to people, *buono* means "good," in the sense of "good in nature." If "good at doing something" is intended, then you must use the adjective *bravo*.

È un buon ragazzo. = He is a good (natured) boy.

È un bravo ragazzo. = He is a good student. (i.e., He is good at being a student.)

Tip

> The forms of *bello* undergo the same kind of changes as the definite article (see §4.2–1) and demonstrative of "farness" (see §4.2–3).
> *bel* corresponds to *il* and *quel*: il giorno / quel giorno / bel giorno
> *bella* corresponds to *la* and *quella*: la giornata / quella giornata / bella giornata
> etc.

BEFORE MASCULINE NOUNS		
	Singular	**Plural**
Beginning with *z*, *s* + consonant, *ps*, *gn*	bello	begli
Beginning with any vowel	bell'	begli
Beginning with any other consonant	bel	bei

BEFORE FEMININE NOUNS		
Beginning with any consonant	bella	belle
Beginning with any vowel	bell'	belle

If placed after the noun, *bello* is treated like a normal descriptive adjective ending in *-o* (see §6.2).

Examples

Singular

un bello sport or *uno sport bello* / a beautiful sport
un bell'orologio or *un orologio bello* / a beautiful watch
un bel fiore or *un fiore bello* / a beautiful flower
una bella donna or *una donna bella* / a beautiful woman
una bell'automobile or *un'automobile bella* / a beautiful automobile

Plural

dei begli sport or *degli sport belli* / some beautiful sports
dei begli orologi or *degli orologi belli* / some beautiful watches
dei bei fiori or *dei fiori belli* / some beautiful flowers
delle belle automobili or *delle automobili belle* /
   some beautiful automobiles

Santo has the following forms when placed before the noun.

BEFORE MASCULINE NOUNS		
	Singular	**Plural**
Beginning with *z*, *s* + consonant, *ps, gn*	santo	
		santi
Beginning with any vowel	sant'	
Beginning with any other consonant	san	
BEFORE FEMININE NOUNS		
Beginning with any consonant	santa	
		sante
Beginning with any vowel	sant'	

Examples

Singular	**Plural**
Santo Stefano / St. Stephen	*i Santi Stefano e Antonio* /
	Saints Stephen and Anthony

San Pietro / St. Peter	*i Santi Pietro e Paolo* / Saints Peter and Paul
Santa Caterina / St. Catharine	*le Sante Caterina e Anna* / Saints Catherine and Anne
Sant'Anna / Saint Anne	*le Sante Anna e Caterina* / Saints Anne and Catherine

Grande has the optional forms *gran* (before a masculine singular noun beginning with any consonant except *z*, *s* + consonant, *ps*, and *gn*), and *grand'* (before any singular noun beginning with a vowel). Otherwise, it is a normal adjective ending in *-e* (see §6.2).

Examples

un gran film or *un grande film* / a great film
un grand'amico or *un grande amico* / a great friend

Note that in the preceding examples, the articles and partitives are changed according to the initial sound of the word they precede—noun or adjective (see §4.2–1, §4.2–2, §4.2–3).

Those adjectives ending in *-co*, *-go*, *-cio*, and *-gio* manifest the same spelling peculiarities when pluralized as the nouns ending in these sounds (see §3.3–4.).

Examples

Singular	Plural
un uomo simpatico / a nice man	*degli uomini simpatici* / some nice men
una strada lunga / a long street	*delle strade lunghe* / some long streets
un vestito grigio / a gray suit	*dei vestiti grigi* / some gray suits

§6.4–2 Interrogative

Gli aggettivi interrogativi

Interrogative adjectives allow us to ask certain types of questions.

Che / what (invariable—never changes its form)

Quale / which	**Singular**	**Plural**
	(Masculine and Feminine)	
	quale	*quali*

quanto / how much, how many		
	Singular	**Plural**
	Masculine:	
	quanto	*quanti*
	Feminine:	
	quanta	*quante*

These adjectives always come before the noun.

Examples

Singular	**Plural**
che	*che*
Che libro leggi? / What book are you reading?	*Che libri leggi?* / What books are you reading?
Che strada è? / What street is it?	*Che strade sono?* / What streets are they?
quale	*quali*
Quale sport preferisci? / Which sport do you prefer?	*Quali sport preferisci?* / Which sports do you prefer?
Quale macchina hai comprato? / Which car did you buy?	*Quali macchine hai comprato?* / Which cars did you buy?
quanto	*quanti*
Quanto zucchero vuoi? / How much sugar do you want?	*Quanti soldi hai?* / How much money do you have?
quanta	*quante*
Quanta minestra vuoi? / How much soup do you want?	*Quante patate mangi?* / How many potatoes are you eating?

§6.4–3 Possessive

> *Gli aggettivi possessivi*

Possessive adjectives allow us to indicate ownership of, or relationship to, something.

Examples

il mio libro / my book (ownership of)
le nostre amiche / our (female) friends (relationship to)

Like all adjectives, possessive adjectives agree in number and gender with the nouns they modify.

	Before Masculine Nouns		Before Feminine Nouns	
	Singular	Plural	Singular	Plural
my	*il mio*	*i miei*	*la mia*	*le mie*
your (familiar, sing.)	*il tuo*	*i tuoi*	*la tua*	*le tue*
his, her, its	*il suo*	*i suoi*	*la sua*	*le sue*
your (polite sing.)	*il Suo*	*i Suoi*	*la Sua*	*le Sue*
our	*il nostro*	*i nostri*	*la nostra*	*le nostre*
your (familiar, pl.)	*il vostro*	*i vostri*	*la vostra*	*le vostre*
their	*il loro*	*i loro*	*la loro*	*le loro*
your (polite, pl.)	*il Loro*	*i Loro*	*la Loro*	*le Loro*

Examples

With Singular Nouns	**With Plural Nouns**
il mio cappotto / my coat	*i miei cappotti* / my coats
la tua bicicletta / your (fam.) bicycle	*le tue biciclette* / your bicycles
il suo biglietto / his, her ticket	*i suoi biglietti* / his, her tickets
la nostra camera / our bedroom	*le nostre camere* / our bedrooms
il vostro passaporto / your (pl.) passport	*i vostri passaporti* / your passports
la loro casa / their house	*le loro case* / their houses
il Suo indirizzo / your (pol.) address	*i Suoi indirizzi* / your addresses
il Loro lavoro / your (pol., pl.) job	*i Loro lavori* / your jobs

As you can see, possessives are adjectives that come before the noun and agree with it in gender and number.

The only invariable form is *loro*: it *never* changes.

Notice that the definite article is part of the possessive adjective. It is, however, dropped for all forms except *loro* when the noun modified has the following characteristics.

It is a kinship noun (i.e., it refers to family members or relatives).

It is singular.

It is unmodified (i.e., it is not accompanied by another adjective, or altered by a suffix—§3.5).

Singular Kinship Noun	**Plural Kinship Noun**
tuo cugino / your cousin	*i tuoi cugini* / your cousins
mia sorella / my sister	*le mie sorelle* / my sisters
nostro fratello / our brother	*i nostri fratelli* / our brothers

Singular Kinship Noun	**Modified or Altered Kinship Noun**
tuo padre / your father	*il tuo padre americano* / your American father
mia sorella / my sister	*la mia sorellina* / my little sister
nostra cugina / our cousin (f.)	*la nostra cugina italiana* / our Italian cousin

The article is always retained with *loro*.

> *il loro figlio* / their son
> *la loro figlia* / their daughter
> *il loro fratello* / their brother

There are a few kinship nouns to which the above rules do not apply, e.g., *mamma* (mom) and *papà* (*babbo*) (dad).

mia madre / my mother	*la mia mamma* / my mom
tuo padre / your father	*il tuo papà* / your dad

Notice that both "his" and "her" are expressed by the same possessive (which takes on the appropriate form before the noun).

His	**Her**
il suo libro / his book	*il suo libro* / her book
i suoi libri / his books	*i suoi libri* / her books
la sua penna / his pen	*la sua penna* / her pen
le sue penne / his pens	*le sue penne* / her pens

Tip

Make the possessive adjective agree with the noun first. Then worry about what it means in English. Otherwise, you will confuse its form with its meaning!

If the noun is masculine singular, use *il suo*
If the noun is feminine singular, use *la sua*
If the noun is masculine plural, use *i suoi*
If the noun is feminine plural, use *le sue*

Notice that "your" has both *familiar* and *polite* forms. More will be said about this distinction in the next chapter (see §7.3–1). As these terms imply, you use familiar forms with the people you know well and with whom you are on familiar terms; otherwise, you use the polite forms.

Note also that the polite forms are identical to the "his, her" forms in the singular, and to the "their" forms in the plural. To keep the two types distinct in writing, the polite forms are often capitalized, as has been done here. But this is *not* an obligatory rule.

> *il suo amico* / his, her friend   *il Suo amico* / your friend
> *le sue cose* / his, her things   *le Sue cose* / your things
> *il loro amico* / their friend   *il Loro amico* / your (pl.) friend
> *le loro cose* / their things   *le Loro cose* / your (pl.) things

Thus, when you see or hear these forms, you will have to figure out what they mean from the context.

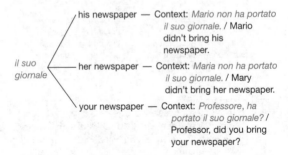

In current Italian, it is not unusual to find only the *vostro* forms used as the plural of both the familiar and polite singular forms.

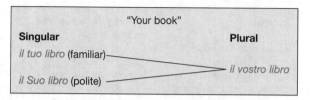

"Your book"

Singular	Plural
il tuo libro (familiar)	
	il vostro libro
il Suo libro (polite)	

The use of *Loro* as the polite plural possessive is restricted to *very* formal situations (see §7.3–1).

The possessive adjective can be put after the noun for emphasis.

È il mio cane. / It's my dog. *È il cane mio! /* It's *my* dog!
Porta tuo cugino. / Bring *Porta il cugino tuo! /* Bring
  your cousin.   *your* cousin!

If the possessive adjective is preceded by the indefinite article, it expresses the formula "of mine," "of yours," etc.

Examples

un mio zio / an uncle of mine
una sua amica / a friend of his, hers

To express "own," use the adjective *proprio*.

il mio proprio cane / my own dog
la (sua) propria chiave / his, her own key

Notice, finally, that the article is dropped when speaking directly to someone.

Mio amico, che fai? / My friend, what are you doing?

§6.4–4 Other Common Adjectives

There are a few other adjectives you should know. Some of these are known as *indefinite* adjectives. The most common are:

Invariable	Like regular adjectives ending in -*o*
abbastanza / enough	*altro* / other
assai / quite, enough	*certo* / certain
ogni / each, every	*molto* / much, many, a lot
qualsiasi / whichever, any	*poco* / little, few
qualunque / whichever, any	*troppo* / too much
	stesso / the same
	ultimo / last
	tutto / all

Examples

Invariable

Non ho abbastanza soldi. / I do not have enough money.

Lui mangia assai carne. / He eats quite a lot of meat.

Ogni mattina leggiamo il giornale. / Every morning we read the newspaper.

In Italia puoi andare a qualsiasi (qualunque) ristorante. / In Italy you can go to any restaurant.

Variable

Chi è l'altra ragazza? / Who is the other girl?

Conosco un certo signore che si chiama Roberto. / I know a certain gentleman named Robert.

Ieri ho mangiato molti (tanti) dolci. / Yesterday I ate a lot of sweets.

Ci sono poche studentesse in questa classe. / There are few female students in this class.

Parecchi turisti visitano Venezia. / A lot of tourists visit Venice.

Abbiamo mangiato troppo gelato. / We ate too much ice cream.

Questa è l'ultima volta che ti telefono. / This is the last time I'm going to call you.

Alcuni, alcune (some), *qualche* (some), and *nessuno* (not . . . any) are technically indefinite adjectives. However, they are used primarily with a partitive function (see §5.2).

Notice that *tutto* is separated from the noun by the definite article.

Examples

> *Lei ha mangiato tutto il riso.* / She ate all the rice.
> *Mario ha mangiato tutta la minestra.* / Mario ate all the soup.

Molto, tanto, poco, and *troppo* are also used as adverbs, in which case there is no agreement. More will be said about this in Chapter 9 (see §9.3).

§6.5 COMPARISON OF ADJECTIVES

Adjectives can be used to indicate that some quality has a relatively equal, greater, or lesser degree of the quality. The three degrees of comparison are *positive, comparative,* and *superlative.*

> For the positive degree use either *così . . . come* or *tanto . . . quanto.*

Examples

> *Paola è così felice come sua sorella.* / Paula is as happy as her sister.
> *Quei ragazzi sono tanto noiosi quanto gli altri.* / Those boys are as boring as the others.

The first words (*così* or *tanto*) are optional.

Examples

> *Paola è felice come sua sorella.*
> *Quei ragazzi sono noiosi quanto gli altri.*

> For the comparative degree simply use *più* (more) or *meno* (less), as the case may be.

Examples

Maria è più studiosa di sua sorella. / Mary is more studious than her sister.

Maria è meno alta di suo fratello. / Mary is shorter than her brother.

Quei ragazzi sono più generosi degli altri. / Those boys are more generous than the others.

Quei ragazzi sono meno intelligenti di quelle ragazze. / Those boys are less intelligent than those girls.

For the superlative degree use the definite article (in its proper form, of course!) followed by *più* or *meno*, as the case may be.

Examples

Maria è la più studiosa della sua classe. / Mary is the most studious in her class.

Quel ragazzo è il più simpatico della famiglia. / That boy is the nicest in this family.

Le patate sono le meno costose. / Potatoes are the least expensive.

In superlative constructions, the definite article is not repeated if it is already in front of a noun.

Examples

Maria è la ragazza più studiosa della classe. / Mary is the most studious girl in the class.

Lui è il ragazzo meno intelligente della classe. / He is the least intelligent boy in the class.

Notice that "in the" is rendered by *di* + definite article (if needed).

Gina è la più elegante della scuola. / Gina is the most elegant in the school.

> *di + la*

Lui è il meno generoso dei miei amici. / He is the least generous of my friends.

> *di + i*

È il ristorante più caro di Roma. / It's the most expensive
restaurant in Rome.

In comparative constructions, the word "than" is rendered
according to the following patterns:

> If two structures (e.g., nouns, substantives, or noun
> phrases) are compared by one adjective, use *di*.

Examples

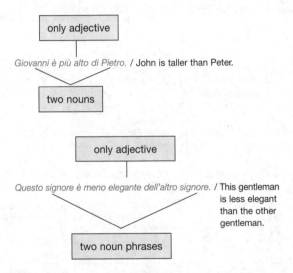

only adjective

Giovanni è più alto di Pietro. / John is taller than Peter.

two nouns

only adjective

Questo signore è meno elegante dell'altro signore. / This gentleman
is less elegant
than the other
gentleman.

two noun phrases

> If two adjectives are used to compare the same structure
> (e.g., a noun, a substantive, or a noun phrase), use *che*.

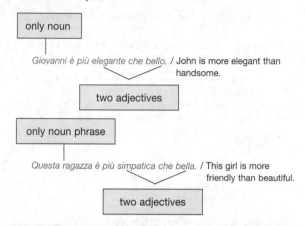

only noun

Giovanni è più elegante che bello. / John is more elegant than handsome.

two adjectives

only noun phrase

Questa ragazza è più simpatica che bella. / This girl is more friendly than beautiful.

two adjectives

If "than what" (= "than that which") is needed, then use *di quello che/di quel che/di ciò che.*

È più intelligente di {quel che} crediamo. / He is more intelligent than we believe.
{quello che}
{ciò che}

Some adjectives have both regular and irregular comparative and superlative forms.

Adjective	Comparative	Superlative
buono / good	*più buono migliore**	*il più buono il migliore*
cattivo / bad	*più cattivo peggiore**	*il più cattivo il peggiore*
grande / big, large	*più grande maggiore**	*il più grande il migliore**
piccolo / small	*più piccolo minore**	*il più piccolo il minore*

Before nouns, the *e* of these forms is normally dropped (e.g., *il miglior vino*; *il peggior vino*).

Examples

> *È il miglior vino della Toscana.* / It's the best wine of Tuscany.
> *Lui è minore di me.* / He is younger (smaller) than I am.

To express "very" as part of the adjective, just drop the final vowel and add *-issimo*. Don't forget to make this newly formed adjective agree with the noun!

Drop the final vowel of the adjective and add *-issimo*:

buono → buon → buonissimo / very good
alto → alt → altissimo / very tall
grande → grand → grandissimo / very big
facile → facil → facilissimo / very easy

Examples

> *Giovanni è intelligentissimo.* / John is very intelligent.
> *Anche Maria è intelligentissima.* / Mary is also very intelligent.
> *Quelle ragazze sono bravissime.* / Those girls are very good.
> *Quelle lezioni sono facilissime.* / Those classes are very easy.

§7.
Pronouns

§7.1 WHAT ARE PRONOUNS?

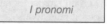

I pronomi

Pronouns are words used in place of nouns, substantives (words taking on the function of nouns), or noun phrases (nouns accompanied by articles, demonstratives, adjectives, etc.).

noun
↓
Giovanni è siciliano. / John is Sicilian.

corresponding
pronoun
↓
Lui è siciliano. / He is Sicilian.

noun phrase
↓
Quel disco nuovo è di Maria. / That new record belongs to Mary.

corresponding
pronoun
↓
Quello è di Maria. / That one belongs to Mary.

§7.2 DEMONSTRATIVE, POSSESSIVE, AND INTERROGATIVE PRONOUNS

> *I pronomi dimostrativi,*
> *possessivi e*
> *interrogativi*

Demonstrative pronouns replace a noun phrase containing a demonstrative adjective (see §4.2–3).

demonstrative   noun
adjective

|
Quel   *ragazzo è italiano.* / That boy is Italian.

|
corresponding
demonstrative
pronoun

|
Quello   *è italiano.* / That one is Italian.

These pronouns correspond to the English demonstrative pronoun phrases "this one," "these ones," "that one," and "those ones."

Demonstrative pronouns take on the gender and number of the noun they replace.

Demonstrative Adjectives	Corresponding Demonstrative Pronouns
"this/these"	"this one/these ones"
With Masculine Nouns Singular	
questo *quest'*	*questo*
Plural	
questi	*questi*
With Feminine Nouns Singular	
questa *quest'*	*questa*
Plural	
queste	*queste*

Demonstrative Adjectives	Corresponding Demonstrative Pronouns
"that/those"	"that one/those ones"
With Masculine Nouns Singular	
quello *quell'* *quel* ——→ *quello*	
Plural	
quegli *quei* ——→ *quelli*	
With Feminine Nouns Singular	
quella *quell'* ——→ *quella*	
Plural	
quelle ——— *quelle*	

Examples

Questo fiore è bello. / This flower is beautiful.
Questo è bello. / This one is beautiful.

Quest'amico è russo. / This friend is Russian.
Questo è russo. / This one is Russian.

Questi dischi sono costosi. / These records are expensive.
Questi sono costosi. / These ones are expensive.

Questa maglia è nuova. / This sweater is new.
Questa è nuova. / This one is new.

Queste banche sono nuove. / These banks are new.
Queste sono nuove. / These ones are new.

Quello studente è canadese. / That student is Canadian.
Quello è canadese. / That one is Canadian.

Quell'amico si chiama Gino. / That friend is called Gino.
Quello si chiama Gino. / That one is called Gino.

Quel ragazzo è spagnolo. / That boy is Spanish.
Quello è spagnolo. / That one is Spanish.

Quegli studenti sono inglesi. / Those students are English.
Quelli sono inglesi. / Those ones are English.

Quei ragazzi sono italiani. / Those boys are Italian.
Quelli sono italiani. / Those ones are Italian.

Quella ragazza è francese. / That girl is French.
Quella è francese. / That one is French.

Quelle studentesse sono francesi. / Those students are French.
Quelle sono francesi. / Those ones are French.

A possessive pronoun replaces a noun phrase containing a possessive adjective (see §6.4–3) and a noun. The Italian possessive pronouns correspond to English "mine," "yours," "his," "hers," "ours," "theirs."

possessive noun
adjective

Il mio fidanzato · *è bello.* / My fiancé is handsome.

corresponding
possessive
pronoun

Il mio · *è bello.* / Mine is handsome.

 Tip

> There is a perfect match between the adjective
> and pronoun forms of the possessive. So, just go
> over the chart in §6.4–3, and it will give you the
> pronoun forms as well.
>
> | **Adjective** | **Pronoun** |
> |---|---|
> | *li mio amico* | *il mio* |
> | *le vostre penne* | *le vostre* |
> | etc. | |

Examples

La sua casa è in Italia. / His, her house is in Italy.
La sua è in Italia. / His, hers is in Italy.

Non mi piacciono i tuoi guanti. / I do not like your gloves.
Non mi piacciono i tuoi. / I do not like yours.

I nostri nonni sono italiani. / Our grandparents are Italian.
I nostri sono italiani. / Ours are Italian.

The article is always used with the pronoun forms, even in the case of singular, unmodified, kinship nouns (review §6.4–3).

Examples

Sua sorella è antipatica. / His, her sister is unpleasant.
La sua è antipatica. / His, hers is unpleasant.

Nostro zio è amichevole. / Our uncle is friendly.
Il nostro è amichevole. / Ours is friendly.

The article can be dropped if the pronoun occurs as a predicate, i.e., if it occurs after the verb *essere* (to be), or some other linking verb (see §6.3).

Examples

> *Questo denaro è mio.* / This money is mine.
> *È tua questa borsa?* / Is this purse yours?
> *Quei biglietti sono suoi.* / Those tickets are his, hers.

An interrogative pronoun replaces a noun or noun phrase introducing a question. The interrogative adjectives discussed in §6.4–2 of the previous chapter have identical pronoun forms.

> The forms *che*, *che cosa*, and *cosa* are synonyms for "what." *Che leggi?* / *Che cosa leggi?* / *Cosa leggi?*

Examples

> *Che libro leggi?* / What book are you reading?
> *Che leggi?* / What are you reading?

The pronouns *quale* ("which") and *quanto* ("how much") agree in number and gender with the noun they replace.

Examples

> *Quali riviste hai comprato?* / Which magazines did you buy?
> *Quali hai comprato?* / Which did you buy?
>
> *Quanti studenti erano presenti?* / How many students were present?
> *Quanti erano presenti?* / How many were present?

Here are other interrogative pronouns:

chi = who, whom *Chi abita a Roma?* / Who lives in Rome? *Chi conosci qui?* / Whom do you know here?
di chi = whose *Di chi è questo portafoglio?* / Whose wallet is this?
a chi = to whom *A chi hai parlato?* / To whom did you speak?
da chi = from whom *Da chi hai comprato la macchina?* / From whom did you buy the car?

The following words are not, strictly speaking, pronouns, but since they allow you to ask questions in exactly the same way, they are listed here for your convenience.

come = how *Come si scrive quella parola?* / How does one write that word?
dove = where *Dove abiti?* / Where do you live?
perché = why *Perché dici così?* / Why do you say that?
quando = when *Quando andrai in Italia?* / When are you going to Italy?

In writing, it is normal to drop the *e* in *come*, *dove*, and *quale* before the verb form *è* (is). For both *come* and *dove* an apostrophe is used. But this is not the case for *quale!*

> *Com'è?* / How is it?
> *Dov'è?* / Where is it?
>
> **BUT**
>
> *Qual è?* / Which is it?

§7.3 PERSONAL PRONOUNS

> *I pronomi personali*

Personal pronouns refer to a person ("I," "you," "we," etc.). They can be classified as subject, object, or reflexive. They are also classified according to the person(s) speaking (= first person), the person(s) spoken to (= second person), or the person(s) spoken about (= third person). The pronoun can, of course, be in the singular (= referring to one person) or in the plural (= referring to more than one person).

§7.3–1 Subject

I pronomi in funzione di soggetto

Subject pronouns are used as the subject of a verb (review the definition of "subject" in §2.1).

Sentence

| Subject Pronoun | Predicate |

Io   *studio il francese.* / I study French.

Loro   *studiano la matematica.* / They study mathematics.

The Italian subject pronouns are:

Person	Italian Forms	English Equivalents	Examples
1st sing.	*io*	I	*Io non capisco.* / I do not understand.
2nd sing.	*tu*	you (familiar)	*Tu sei simpatico.* / You are nice.
3rd sing.	*lui*	he	*Lui è americano.* / He is American.
	lei	she	*Lei è americana.* / She is American.
	Lei	you (polite)	*Come si chiama, Lei?* / What is your name?

Person	Italian Forms	English Equivalents	Examples
1st pl.	*noi*	we	*Noi non lo conosciamo./* We do not know him.
2nd pl.	*voi*	you	*Voi arrivate sempre in ritardo.* / You always arrive late.
3rd pl.	*loro*	they	*Loro vanno in Italia.* / They are going to Italy.
	Loro	you (formal)	*Come si chiamano, Loro?* / What is your name?

Notice that *io* (I) is not capitalized (unless it is the first word of a sentence).

Subject pronouns are optional in formal affirmative sentences (see §2.2–1) because it is easy to tell from the verb ending which person is referred to.

> *Io non capisco.* or *Non capisco.* / I do not understand.
> *Loro vanno in Italia.* or *Vanno in Italia.* / They are going to Italy.

Sometimes, however, the way a sentence is constructed makes it impossible to avoid using pronouns. This is particularly true when you want to emphasize the subject.

Examples

> *Devi parlare tu, non io!* / You have to speak, not I!
> *Non è possibile che l'abbiano fatto loro.* / It's not possible that they did it.

These pronouns must also be used to avoid confusion when more than one person is being referred to.

Examples

Mentre lui guarda la TV, lei ascolta la radio. / While he watches
    TV, she listens to the radio.
Lui e io vogliamo che tu dica la verità. / He and I want you to tell
    the truth.

They are used after the words *anche* (also, too) and *neanche*
(neither, not even) (whose synonyms are *neppure* and *nem-
meno*), and *proprio* (really).

Examples

Anche tu devi venire alla festa. / You too must come to the
    party.
Non è venuto neanche lui. / He didn't come either.
Signor Bianchi, è proprio Lei? / Mr. Bianchi, is it really you?

The subject pronoun "it" usually is not stated in Italian.

Examples

È vero. / It is true.
Pare che sia corretto. / It appears to be correct.

However, if you should ever need to express this subject, use
esso (m.), *essa* (f.); and plural forms *essi* (m.), *esse* (f.).

È una buona scusa, ma neanche essa potrà aiutarti adesso. / It's
    a good excuse, but not even it can help you now.

Tip

> Notice that "you" has both familiar and polite
> forms. These are not optional! If you address
> someone incorrectly, it might be taken as rude-
> ness! So, be careful.
>
> The familiar forms (and their corresponding verb
> forms) are used, as the name suggests, with peo-
> ple with whom you are on familiar terms, that is,
> members of the family, friends, etc. If you call
> someone by a first name, then you are obviously
> on familiar terms.

Examples

Maria, anche tu studi l'italiano? / Mary, are you studying Italian too?
Signora Bianchi, anche Lei studia l'italiano? / Mrs. Bianchi, are
    you studying Italian too?

In writing, the polite forms (*Lei, Loro*) are often capitalized in
order to distinguish them from *lei* (she) and *loro* (they), but this
is not obligatory.

In the plural, there is a strong tendency in current Italian to
use *voi* as the plural of both *tu* and *Lei*. *Loro* is restricted to
very formal situations (when addressing an audience, when a
waiter takes an order, etc.)

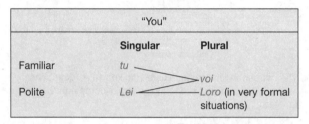

	"You"	
	Singular	**Plural**
Familiar	*tu*	
		voi
Polite	*Lei*	*Loro* (in very formal situations)

The forms *lui* (he) and *lei* (she) are used in ordinary conversation. However, there are two more formal pronouns: *egli* (he)
and *ella* (she).

Normal Conversational Italian
Giovanni è italiano, ma neanche lui capisce i pronomi! / John is
    Italian, but he doesn't understand pronouns either!

Formal (Usually Written) Italian
Dante scrisse la Divina Commedia. Egli era fiorentino. / Dante
    wrote the *Divine Comedy*. He was Florentine.

§7.3–2 Object

> *I pronomi in funzione di*
> *complemento (oggetto)*

Object pronouns are used as objects of verbs. As discussed in Chapter 2 (review section §2.2–1), the object can be direct or indirect.

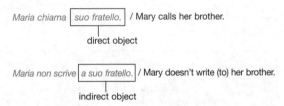

Maria chiama suo fratello. / Mary calls her brother.

direct object

Maria non scrive a suo fratello. / Mary doesn't write (to) her brother.

indirect object

The corresponding pronouns are also known as direct and indirect. Italian object pronouns generally come right *before* the verb.

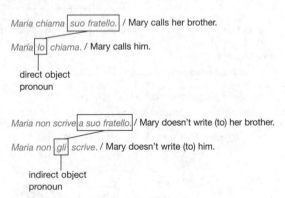

Maria chiama suo fratello. / Mary calls her brother.

Maria lo *chiama.* / Mary calls him.

direct object
pronoun

Maria non scrive a suo fratello. / Mary doesn't write (to) her brother.

Maria non gli *scrive.* / Mary doesn't write (to) him.

indirect object
pronoun

The Italian object pronouns are detailed in the charts below.

> **Tip**
>
> Notice that the first and second person pronouns are identical. Differences occur only in the third person.
>
> *mi* = both "me" and "to me"
> *ti* = both "you" and "to you"
> but
> *lo* = "him" and *gli* = "to him"
> etc.

The Italian object pronouns are detailed in the charts below. As mentioned in the previous section (see §7.3–1), there are both familiar and polite forms in the singular, but in the plural there is a tendency to use only the second person familiar form.

	Singular	**Plural**
Familiar	*ti*	
Polite	*La* (direct)	*vi*
	Le (indirect)	

Person	Object Pronouns		Examples
	Direct	**Indirect**	
1st sing.	*mi* (me)	*mi* (to me)	*Maria mi chiama.* / Mary calls me. *Maria mi scrive.* / Mary writes (to) me.
2nd sing. fam.	*ti* (you)	*ti* (to you)	*Ti chiamo fra mezz'ora.* / I'll call you in a half hour. *Ti scrivo fra un mese.* / I'll write (to) you in a month.

Person	Object Pronouns		Examples
	Direct	Indirect	
3rd sing.	*lo* (m.) (him)	*gli* (m.) (to him)	*Maria lo chiama.* / Mary calls him. *Maria gli scrive spesso.* / Mary writes (to) him often.
	la (f.) (her)	*le* (f.) (to her)	*Maria la chiama.* / Mary calls her. *Maria le scrive spesso.* / Mary writes (to) her often.
polite	*La* (you)	*Le* (to you)	*Signore, La chiamo domani.* / Sir, I'll call you tomorrow. *Signore, Le scrivo fra un mese.* / Sir, I'll write (to) you in a month.
1st pl.	*ci* (us)	*ci* (to us)	*Perché non ci chiami?* / Why don't you call us? *Perché non ci scrivi?* / Why don't you write to us?
2nd pl.	*vi* (you)	*vi* (to you)	*Domani vi chiamo.* / Tomorrow I'll call you. *Vi scrivo dall'Italia.* / I'll write (to) you from Italy.
3rd pl.	*li* (m.) *le* (f.) (them)	*gli* (m.) *gli* (f.) (to them)	*Li chiamo dopo.* / I'll call them (m.) after. *Le chiamo dopo.* / I'll call them (f.) after. *Maria e Claudia? Non gli scrivo più.* / Mary and Claudia? I don't write to them (f.) anymore. *Gianni e Paolo? Non gli scrivo più.* / Johhny and Paul? I don't write to them (m.) anymore.

Notice that the plural of the indirect object pronouns *gli* (to him) and *le* (to her) is *gli* (to them). This is very common in current ordinary Italian. However, in more formal situations, some Italians prefer to use *loro* (to them), which goes *after* the verb.

Examples

Normal Usage	**Very Formal Usage**
I ragazzi? Gli parlo domani. / The boys? I'll speak to them tomorrow.	*I signori? Parlo loro domani.* / The gentlemen? I'll speak to them tomorrow.
Le ragazze? Gli parlo domani. / The girls? I'll speak to them tomorrow.	*Le signore? Parlo loro domani.* / The ladies? I'll speak to them tomorrow.

The English direct object pronoun "it" (plural, "them") is expressed by the third person direct object pronoun. Be careful! Choose the pronoun according to the gender and number of the noun it replaces.

Examples

Giovanni compra il biglietto. / John is buying the ticket.

Giovanni lo compra. / John is buying it.

Giovanni compra i biglietti. / John is buying the tickets.

Giovanni li compra. / John is buying them.

Giovanni compra la rivista. / John is buying the magazine.

Giovanni la compra. / John is buying it.

Giovanni compra le riviste. / John is buying the magazines.

Giovanni le compra. / John is buying them.

The past participle of the verb agrees in gender and number with these four pronouns (*lo*, *la*, *li*, *le*) (see Chapter 8 for verb forms using the past participle).

Examples

Giovanni ha comprato il biglietto. / John bought the ticket.

Giovanni lo ha comprato. / John bought it.

Giovanni ha comprato i biglietti. / John bought the tickets.

Giovanni li ha comprati. / John bought them.

Giovanni ha comprato la rivista. / John bought the magazine.

Giovanni la ha comprata. / John bought it.

Giovanni ha comprato le riviste. / John bought the magazines.

Giovanni le ha comprate. / John bought them.

Note that only the singular forms *lo* and *la* can be elided with the auxiliary forms of *avere: ho, hai, ha, hanno* (see §8.2–2).

> *Giovanni lo ha comprato.* or *Giovanni l'ha comprato.* / John bought it.
> *Giovanni la ha comprata.* or *Giovanni l'ha comprata.* / John bought it.

Agreement with the other direct object pronouns *mi, ti, ci, vi* is optional.

Giovanni ci ha chiamato. / John called us.

or

Giovanni ci ha chiamati. / John phoned us.

There is *no* agreement with indirect object pronouns.

Giovanni gli ha scritto. / John wrote (to) him, (to) them.
Giovanni le ha scritto. / John wrote (to) her.

But be very careful! The pronoun form *le* has two meanings.

Direct Object *le* = **them**
Giovanni ha mandato le lettere. / John sent the letters.
Giovanni le ha mandate. / John sent them.

Indirect Object *le* = **to her**
Giovanni ha scritto a Maria. / John wrote (to) Mary.
Giovanni le ha scritto. / John wrote (to) her.

Direct object pronouns normally follow an infinitive or gerund and are attached to it (see §8.6–1 and §8.6–2). In that case, you must drop the final -*e* of the infinitive:

> *parlare:* → *parlar* → *parlarmi, parlarti,* etc.
>
> *Prima di mangiare il vitello, prenderò i tortellini.* / Before eating the veal, I'm going to have the tortellini.
>
> *Prima di mangiarlo, prenderò i tortellini.* / Before eating it, I'm going to have the tortellini.
>
> *Vedendo Maria, l'ho salutata.* / Seeing Mary, I greeted her.
>
> *Vedendola, l'ho salutata.* / Seeing her, I greeted her.

They are also attached to the form *ecco* (here is, here are, there is, there are) (see §11.3).

> *Ecco la ricetta.* / Here is the recipe.
>
> *Eccola.* / Here it is.
>
> *Ecco i nostri genitori.* / Here are our parents.
>
> *Eccoli.* / Here they are.

With *modal* verbs such as *potere* (to be able to), *dovere* (to have to), and *volere* (to want) (see §8.9), you can either attach the object pronoun to the infinitive, or put it before the modal.

Maria non può mangiare il pollo. / Mary can't eat chicken.

Maria non lo può mangiare. / Mary can't eat it.

or

Maria non può mangiarlo. / Mary can't eat it.

Gli studenti devono studiare i pronomi. / The students have to study the pronouns.

Gli studenti li devono studiare.

or

Gli studenti devono studiarli. / The students have to study them.

These pronouns are attached to the familiar forms of the imperative (see §8.3).

Giovanni, paga il conto! / John, pay the bill!

Giovanni, pagalo! / John, pay it!

But with polite forms:

Signor Verdi, paghi il conto! / Mr. Verdi, pay the bill!

Signor Verdi, lo paghi! / Mr. Verdi, pay it!

Now comes the complicated task of sequencing indirect and direct objects. Just remember the following, and you won't have too much difficulty.

The indirect object always precedes the direct object (*lo*, *la*, *li*, or *le*).

Giovanni me lo dà. / John gives it to me.

indirect   direct
object   object

> Change the indirect forms *mi*, *ti*, *ci*, and *vi* to *me*, *te*, *ce*, and *ve*, respectively.

Giovanni mi dà l'indirizzo. / John gives me the address.

Giovanni me lo dà. / John gives it to me.

Giovanni ti manda i francobolli. / John sends you the stamps.

Giovanni te li manda. / John sends them to you.

Giovanni ci scrive una cartolina. / John writes us a card.

Giovanni ce la scrive. / John writes it to us.

Giovanni vi scrive una cartolina. / John writes you a card.

Giovanni ve la scrive. / John writes it to you.

> Change the indirect forms *gli* and *le* to *glie*, and combine this with *lo*, *la*, *li*, or *le* to form one word: *glielo*, *gliela*, *glieli*, *gliele*

Lo studente gli porta gli esercizi. / The student brings the exercises to him, them.

Lo studente glieli porta. / The student brings them to him, them.

Lo studente le porta le dispense. / The student brings the course notes to her.

Lo studente gliele porta. / The student brings them to her.

When the pronouns are attached to a verb (in the cases discussed above), they are always written as one word.

Prima di mandarti la lettera, ti telefono. / Before sending you the letter, I'll phone you.

Prima di mandartela, ti telefono. / Before sending it to you, I'll phone you.

Giovanni, paga <u>il conto</u> <u>al cameriere</u>! / John, pay the bill to the waiter!

Giovanni, paga<u>glielo</u>! / John, pay it to him!

Maria deve comprar<u>mi</u> <u>una borsa</u>. / Mary has to buy me a purse.

Maria deve comprar<u>mela</u>. / Mary has to buy it for me.

And do not forget that when *lo*, *la*, *li*, *le* are put before a past participle, there must be agreement.

Lo studente <u>gliele</u> ha portate. / The student brought them to her.

The forms *glielo* and *gliela* can be elided with the auxiliary forms *ho*, *hai*, *ha*, *hanno*.

Gliel'hanno portato. / They bought it to him, her, them.

There is a second type of object pronoun that goes after the verb. It is known as a *stressed* or *tonic* pronoun.

Before Verb	After Verb	Translation
mi	*me*	me
mi	*a me*	to me
ti	*te*	you (fam., sing.)
ti	*a te*	to you (fam., sing.)
lo	*lui*	him
gli	*a lui*	to him
la	*lei*	her/you (pol.)
lei	*a lei*	to her/to you (pol.)
ci	*noi*	us
ci	*a noi*	to us
vi	*voi*	you (pl.)
vi	*a voi*	to you (pl.)
li	*loro*	them (m.)
gli	*loro*	to them (m.)
le	*loro*	them (f.)
gli	*loro*	to them (f.)

These allow you to put greater emphasis on the object.

Examples

Normal Speech	**Emphasis**
Maria mi chiama. / Mary calls me.	*Maria chiama me, non te!* / Mary calls me, not you!
Giovanni gli dice la verità. / John tells him the truth.	*Giovanni dice la verità a lui, non a loro!* / John tells him, not them, the truth!

They also allow you to be precise and clear about the person you are referring to.

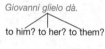

Giovanni glielo dà.

to him? to her? to them?

Giovanni lo dà a lui. / John gives it to him.

Giovanni lo dà a lei. / John gives it to her.

Giovanni lo dà a loro. / John gives it to them.

These are the *only* object pronouns you can use after a preposition.

Examples

Maria viene con noi. / Mary is coming with us.
Il professore parla di te. / The professor is speaking of you.
L'ha fatto per me. / He did it for me.

Tip

> In most situations, use the pronouns that come before the verb (or are attached to infinitives and gerunds), also known as *unstressed object pronouns*. However, if you want to add an element of emphasis, or you want to make sure your message is clear and unambiguous, use the *stressed object pronouns*.

§7.3–3 Reflexive

> *I pronomi riflessivi*

Reflexive pronouns "reflect" the subject of a verb. Like object pronouns, they generally come before the verb.

La ragazza si lava prima di andare a dormire.

The girl washes herself before going to sleep.

The Italian reflexive pronouns are:

Person	Italian Forms	English Equivalents	Examples
1st sing.	*mi*	myself	*Io mi lavo.* / I wash myself.
2nd sing. familiar	*ti*	yourself	*Tu ti diverti.* / You enjoy yourself.
3rd sing.	*si*	himself, herself, oneself, itself	*Lui si diverte.* / He enjoys himself. *Anche lei si diverte.* / She enjoys herself too.
3rd sing.	*Si*	yourself (pol.)	*Si diverte, Lei?* / Are you enjoying yourself?
1st pl.	*ci*	ourselves	*Anche noi ci divertiamo.* / We too are enjoying ourselves.
2nd pl.	*vi*	yourselves	*Vi divertite, voi?* / Are you enjoying yourselves?
3rd pl.	*si*	themselves	*Loro si divertono sempre.* / They always enjoy themselves.
3rd pl.	*Si*	yourselves (pol.)	*Si divertono, Loro?* / Are you enjoying yourselves?

Notice that the third person polite forms of address are often capitalized to distinguish them from the other third person forms in writing (see also §7.3–1).

These pronouns are also used as *reciprocal forms:* "to each other," "to themselves," etc.

> *Si telefonano ogni sera.* / They phone each other every night.
> *Noi ci scriviamo ogni mese.* / We write each other every month.

After prepositions (especially *da*), the stressed forms *me, te, sé, noi, voi* are used instead.

> *Ci vado da me.* / I'm going there by myself.
> *Lo farà da sé.* / He'll do it by himself.

Notice that *sé* is written with an accent. However, in the expression *se stesso* (by oneself) the accent is omitted.

> *Ci andrà se stesso.* / He'll go by himself.
> *Maria gli scriverà se stessa.* / Mary will write to him herself.

For more information on these pronouns, see §8.7.

§7.4   RELATIVE PRONOUNS

> *I pronomi relativi*

As discussed in Chapter 2 (review §2.3–1), a relative clause is introduced into a main sentence by means of a *relative* pronoun, which serves as a subject or an object in the clause. The relative pronouns in Italian are:

> *che* / that, which, who
>
> After a preposition:
>
> *cui* / which, of whom, to whom, etc.
>
> *chi* / he who, she who, they who
>
> *quel che* / that which
> *quello che* / that which
> *ciò che* / that which

Examples

che

Quella donna che legge il giornale è mia sorella. / That woman
who is reading the newspaper is my sister.

Il vestito che ho comprato ieri è molto bello. / The dress I bought
yesterday is very beautiful.

Mi piace la poesia che stai leggendo. / I like the poem (that) you
are reading.

cui

Il ragazzo a cui ho dato il regalo è mio cugino. / The boy to whom
I gave the gift is my cousin.

Non trovo il cassetto in cui ho messo il mio anello. / I can't find
the drawer in which I put my ring.

Ecco la rivista di cui ho parlato. / Here is the magazine of which I
spoke.

chi

Chi va in Italia si divertirà. / He, she who goes to Italy will enjoy
himself, herself.

C'è chi dorme e c'è chi lavora. / Some sleep, some work! (*lit.*,
There is he who sleeps and there is he who works!)

quel che /quello che /ciò che

Quello che dici è vero. / What (that which) you are saying is true.

Non sai quel che dici. / You don't know what you are saying.

Ciò che dici non ha senso. / What you are saying makes no sense.

Both *che* and *cui* can be replaced by *il quale* if there is an
antecedent. It changes in form according to the noun it refers
to and is always preceded by the definite article.

L'uomo che legge il giornale è italiano. / The man who is reading
the newspaper is Italian.

or

L'uomo il quale legge il giornale è italiano. / The man who is reading the newspaper is Italian.

Gli uomini che leggono il giornale sono italiani. / The men who are
reading the newspaper are Italian.

or

Gli uomini i quali leggono il giornale sono italiani. / The men who
are reading the newspaper are Italian.

La donna che legge il giornale è italiana. / The woman who is
reading the newspaper is Italian.

or

La donna la quale legge il giornale è italiana. / The woman who is
reading the newspaper is Italian.

Le donne che leggono il giornale sono italiane. / The women who
are reading the newspaper are Italian.

or

Le donne le quali leggono il giornale sono italiane. / The women
who are reading the newspaper are Italian.

The form *il cui* is used to convey "whose." The article varies
according to the gender and number of the noun modified.

Ecco il professore il cui corso è molto interessante. / Here is the
professor whose course is very interesting.

Ecco gli scrittori i cui romanzi sono celebri. / Here are the writers
whose novels are famous.

Ecco la ragazza la cui intelligenza è straordinaria. / Here is the girl
whose intelligence is extraordinary.

Ecco la ragazza le cui amiche sono italiane. / Here is the girl
whose friends are Italian.

§7.5 OTHER PRONOUNS

The indefinite adjectives discussed in Chapter 6 have corresponding indefinite pronouns. These are invariable (review the chart in §6.4–4).

Examples

Lui mangia assai. / He eats quite a lot.
Tuo fratello dorme molto, no? / Your brother sleeps a lot, doesn't he?
Ieri ho mangiato troppo. / Yesterday I ate too much.

When referring to people in general, use the plural forms *molti, alcuni, tanti, pochi, parecchi, tutti,* etc.

Examples

Molti vanno in Italia quest'anno. / Many are going to Italy this year.
Alcuni dormono alla mattina, ma parecchi lavorano già. / Some sleep in the morning, but quite a few are working already.
Tutti sanno quello. / Everyone knows that.

Use the corresponding feminine forms (*molte, alcune,* etc.) when referring only to females.

Examples

Di quelle ragazze, molte sono italiane. / Of those girls, many are Italian.
Di tutte quelle donne, alcune sono americane. / Of all those women, some are American.

Notice the expression *alcuni . . . altri* (some . . . others).

Alcuni andranno in Italia; altri, invece, andranno in Francia. / Some will go to Italy; others, instead, will go to France.

The pronoun *ne* has four main functions. It is used to replace:

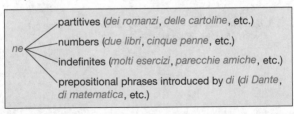

ne
— partitives (*dei romanzi, delle cartoline,* etc.)
— numbers (*due libri, cinque penne,* etc.)
— indefinites (*molti esercizi, parecchie amiche,* etc.)
— prepositional phrases introduced by *di* (*di Dante, di matematica,* etc.)

Like most object pronouns, it is usually placed before the verb (except in those cases discussed in §7.3–2).

Examples

ne = "some" (partitives)

Domani scriverò <u>delle cartoline</u>. / Tomorrow I'm going to write some postcards.

Domani <u>ne</u> scriverò. / Tomorrow I'm going to write some.

Anch'io devo comprare <u>della carne</u>. / I too have to buy some meat.

Anch'io <u>ne</u> devo comprare. / I too have to buy some.

ne = "of them" (numbers)

Domani comprerò <u>tre matite</u>. / Tomorrow I will buy three pencils.

Domani <u>ne</u> comprerò <u>tre</u>. / Tomorrow I will buy three (of them).

Voglio comprare <u>quattro dischi</u>. / I want to buy four records.

<u>Ne</u> voglio comprare <u>quattro</u>. / I want to buy four (of them).

ne = "of them" (indefinites)

Domani vedrò <u>molte amiche</u>. / Tomorrow I'm going to see many (female) friends.

Domani <u>ne</u> vedrò <u>molte</u>. / Tomorrow I'm going to see many of them.

Devo comprare <u>parecchi regali</u>. / I have to buy quite a few presents.

<u>Ne</u> devo comprare <u>parecchi</u>. / I have to buy quite a few of them.

ne = "of it, them" (phrases)

Il professore parlerà <u>di matematica</u>. / The professor will speak about mathematics.

Il professore <u>ne</u> parlerà. / The professor will speak about it.

Lei parlerà <u>del suo amico</u>. / She will speak about her friend.

Lei <u>ne</u> parlerà. / She will speak about him.

When *ne* replaces partitives, numbers, and indefinites, there is agreement between *ne* and the past participle. This is not the case when *ne* replaces a prepositional phrase introduced by *di*.

> *Ha comprato <u>dei dolci</u>.* / He bought some sweets.
>
> *<u>Ne</u> ha comprati.* / He bought some.
>
> *Ha veduto <u>tre film</u>.* / He saw three films.
>
> *<u>Ne</u> ha veduti tre.* / He saw three (of them).
>
> *Ha mangiato <u>molta pasta</u>.* / He ate a lot of pasta.
>
> *<u>Ne</u> ha mangiata molta.* / He ate a lot (of it).

> But

> *Ha parlato <u>di quella ragazza</u>.* / He spoke about that girl.
>
> *<u>Ne</u> ha parlato.* / He spoke about her.

The locative (place) pronoun *ci* means "there." Like other unstressed pronouns, it goes before the verb (except in the cases mentioned in §7.3–2).

> *ci* = "there"
>
> *Andiamo <u>in Inghilterra</u> domani.* / We are going to England tomorrow.
>
> *<u>Ci</u> andiamo domani.* / We are going there tomorrow.
>
> *Chi abita <u>in quella città</u>?* / Who lives in that city?
>
> *Chi <u>ci</u> abita?* / Who lives there?

However, to express "from there," you have to use *ne* (again!).

> *Tu vai <u>in Italia</u>, e io vengo <u>dall'Italia</u>.* / You are going to Italy, and I'm coming from Italy.
>
> *Tu <u>ci</u> vai, e io <u>ne</u> vengo.* / You are going there, and I'm coming from there.

In these cases, there is no agreement between *ci* and *ne* and the past participle.

Both *ci* and *ne* can occur in sequence with object pronouns.

Ci is changed to *ce* when it precedes other pronouns.

Io metto il portafoglio <u>nel cassetto</u>. / I put my wallet in the drawer.

Chi <u>ce</u> lo mette? / Who is putting it there?

Ne is placed after the indirect object pronouns in the normal fashion.

Giovanni mi dà <u>delle rose</u>. / John gives me some roses.

Giovanni me <u>ne</u> dà. / John gives some to me.

Il medico gli dà <u>delle pillole</u>. / The doctor gives him some pills.

Il medico glie<u>ne</u> dà. / The doctor gives some to him.

And now for the last pronoun to be discussed! The impersonal *si* (one in general, we, they, etc.) has the following peculiar characteristics:

Unlike its synonym *uno*, with *si* the verb agrees with what appears to be the predicate.

Uno compra quel libro solo in Italia. / One buys that book only in Italy.

or

Si compra quel libro solo in Italia. / One buys that book only in Italy.

Uno compra quei libri solo in Italia. / One buys those books only in Italy.

or

Si comprano quei libri solo in Italia. / One buys those books only in Italy.

All compound tenses using *si* (see §8.2–2), are conjugated with *essere* (to be), with the past participle agreeing, apparently, with the predicate!

> *Abbiamo veduto quei film solo in Italia.* / We have seen those films only in Italy.
>
> or
>
> *Si sono veduti quei film solo in Italia.* / We have seen those films only in Italy.

When followed by a predicate adjective (see §6.3), the adjective is always in the plural.

> *Siamo contenti in Italia.* / We are happy in Italy.
>
> or
>
> *Si è contenti in Italia.* / We are happy in Italy.

Direct object pronouns are placed before it!

> *Uno deve dire la verità.* / One has to tell the truth.
> *Uno la deve dire.* / One has to tell it.
>
> or
>
> *La si deve dire.* / One has to tell it.

In front of the reflexive *si* (see §7.3–3), "oneself," *si* changes to *ci!*

> *Uno si diverte in Italia.* / One enjoys oneself in Italy.
> *Ci si diverte in Italia.* / One enjoys oneself in Italy.

Tip

As you have seen, the pronoun system of Italian is a complex and large one. One good way to grasp the system is to work on the forms that have many meanings and functions.

Take, as an example, *si*. By reading the appropriate sections of this chapter, you can make an appropriate list of its meanings and functions as follows:

As a reflexive pronoun

"himself" as in:
Lui si diverte. / He enjoys himself.

"herself" as in:
Lei si diverte. / She enjoys herself.

"yourself" (pol.) as in:

Signora Verdi, Lei si diverte? / Mrs. Verdi, are you enjoying yourself?

As an impersonal form

Si mangia bene in Italia. / One eats well in Italy.
Ci si può divertire in Italia. / One can enjoy oneself in Italy.
etc.

§8.
Verbs

§8.1 WHAT ARE VERBS?

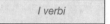

I verbi

Verbs are words that indicate the action performed by the subject of a sentence. For this reason, they agree with the subject's *person* (first, second, third; see §7.3) and *number* (singular or plural).

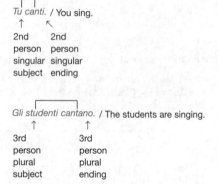

Tu canti. / You sing.

2nd   2nd
person person
singular singular
subject ending

Gli studenti cantano. / The students are singing.

3rd   3rd
person person
plural plural
subject ending

For the kinds of objects that verbs can take, go over §2.2–1. In an Italian dictionary a verb is listed in its infinitive form (see §8.6–1). Italian verbs are divided into three conjugations according to their infinitive endings.

parl are / to speak   *mett* ere / to put   *dorm* ire / to sleep
    ↑   ↑   ↑

first   second   third
conjugation   conjugation   conjugation
infinitive   infinitive   infinitive
ending   ending   ending

Tip

These infinitive endings allow you to determine which person and number endings a verb must take when you conjugate it (that is, when you attach the endings to the verb according to a conjugation pattern.)

A verb tense indicates the time the action occurred: *now* (present tense), *before* (past tense), or *after* (future tense).

La mangio adesso. / I'm eating it now. (present tense)
L'ho mangiata ieri. / I ate it yesterday. (past tense)
La mangerò domani. / I will eat it tomorrow. (future tense)

Not only do verbs allow you to express a time relationship, but they also allow you to convey manner of thinking, point of view, etc. This characteristic of a verb is known as its *mood*.

Maria scrive la lettera. / Mary is writing the letter. (indicative mood = statement)
Maria, scrivi la lettera! / Mary, write the letter! (imperative mood = command)
È probabile che Maria scriva la lettera. / It's probable that Mary is writing the letter. (subjunctive mood = probability)

A *regular verb* is one whose conjugation follows a systematic pattern. A verb that does not is known as *irregular*. You will find some common irregular verbs in the *Verb Charts* section at the back of this book.

§8.2 THE INDICATIVE TENSES

The *indicative* mood allows you to express or indicate facts. It is used for ordinary statements and questions. It is the most commonly used mood in everyday conversation.

§8.2–1 Present

> *Il presente dell'indicativo*

To form the present indicative, do the following:

> Drop the infinitive ending of the verb.
> *parlare* → *parl-* / to speak
> *scrivere* → *scriv-* / to write
> *aprire* → *apr-* / to open
> *capire* → *cap-* / to understand

Add the following endings to the stem according to the conjugation.

Person	Endings		
	1st Conjugation = are	**2nd Conjugation** = ere	**3rd Conjugation** = ire
1st sing. (io)	*-o*	*-o*	*-o / -isco*
2nd sing. (tu)	*-i*	*-i*	*-i / -isci*
3rd sing. (lui/lei)	*-a*	*-e*	*-e / -isce*
1st pl. (noi)	*-iamo*	*-iamo*	*-iamo / -iamo*
2nd pl. (voi)	*-ate*	*-ete*	*-ite / -ite*
3rd pl. (loro)	*-ano*	*-ono*	*-ono / -iscono*

Conjugations

parlare → *parl-*

(io)	*parlo*/	I speak, I am speaking, I do speak
(tu)	*parli*/	you speak, you are speaking, you do speak
(lui/lei)	*parla*/	he, she, you (pol.) speak(s), he, she, you (pol.) is/ are speaking, he, she, you (pol.) does/do speak
(noi)	*parliamo*/	we speak, we are speaking, we do speak
(voi)	*parlate*/	you speak, you are speaking, you do speak
(loro)	*parlano*/	they speak, they are speaking, they do speak

scrivere → *scriv-*

(io)	*scrivo*/	I write, I am writing, I do write
(tu)	*scrivi*/	you write, you are writing, you do write
(lui/lei)	*scrive*/	he, she, you (pol.) write(s), he, she, you (pol.) is/ are writing, he, she, you (pol.) does/do write
(noi)	*scriviamo*/	we write, we are writing, we do write
(voi)	*scrivete*/	you write, you are writing, you do write
(loro)	*scrivono*/	they write, they are writing, they do write

aprire → *apr-*

(io)	*apro*/	I open, I am opening, I do open
(tu)	*apri*/	you open, you are opening, you do open
(lui/lei)	*apre*/	he, she, you (pol.) open(s), he, she, you (pol.) is/are opening, he, she, you (pol.) does/do open
(noi)	*apriamo*/	we open, we are opening, we do open
(voi)	*aprite*/	you open, you are opening, you do open
(loro)	*aprono*/	they open, they are opening, they do open

capire → *cap-*

(io)	*capisco*/	I understand, I do understand
(tu)	*capisci*/	you understand, you do understand
(lui/lei)	*capisce*/	he, she, you (pol.) understand(s), he, she, you (pol.) does/do understand
(noi)	*capiamo*/	we understand, we do understand
(voi)	*capite*/	you understand, you do understand
(loro)	*capiscono*/	they understand, they do understand

Examples

Lui parla molto bene./ He speaks very well.

Quando scrivi quella lettera?/ When are you writing that letter?

Non apriamo mai le finestre d'inverno./ We never open the windows in the winter.

È vero; lei scrive molto bene. / It's true; she does write very well.
Gli studenti non capiscono la lezione. / The students do not
    understand the lesson.
Finisco di lavorare alle sei. / I finish working at six.
Quale preferisce, Lei? / Which one do you (pol.) prefer?
Loro dormono troppo. / They sleep too much.
A che ora partite domani? /
    At what time are you leaving tomorrow?

Note that there are two sets of endings in the third conjugation. Two other verbs conjugated like *aprire* are:

dormire / to sleep
partire / to leave

Two other verbs conjugated like *capire* are:

finire / to finish
preferire / to prefer

You will have to learn whether a given third conjugation verb
follows this pattern or the other one (*aprire*). A good dictionary
will provide this kind of information.

> **Tip**
>
> Be careful when you pronounce the third person
> plural forms! The accent is *not* placed on the
> ending.
> *parlano* / they speak   *scrivono* / they write
> | |
> stress   stress

Recall from the previous chapter (see §7.3–1) that subject
pronouns are optional with the indicative tenses. The reason
for this is obvious: the endings make it clear which person is
being referred to.

The third person forms are also used, of course, with subjects that are not pronouns.

Quella ragazza studia molto. / That girl studies a lot.
Quegli studenti non studiano mai. / Those students never study.

Remember as well (§7.3–1) that for the singular polite "you," the third person singular form is used.

Cosa preferisci, tu? / What do you (fam.) prefer?
Cosa preferisce, Lei? / What do you (pol.) prefer?

And do not forget that the subject pronoun "it" (plural "they") is not normally expressed (§7.3–1).

Apre a mezzogiorno. / It opens at noon.

In the first conjugation, if a verb ends in *-care* or *-gare*, then you indicate the hard sound by using an *h* before the endings *-i* and *-iamo*.

cercare / to search for	*pagare* / to pay (for)
(io) cerco / I search	*(io) pago* / I pay
(tu) cerchi / you search	*(tu) paghi* / you pay
(lui/lei) cerca / he, she, it searches	*(lui/lei) paga* / he, she, it pays
(noi) cerchiamo / we search	*(noi) paghiamo* / we pay
(voi) cercate / you search	*(voi) pagate* / you pay
(loro) cercano / they search	*(loro) pagano* / they pay

Also in the first conjugation, if a verb ends in *-ciare* and *-giare*, then you do not need to keep the *-i* of these endings before the *-i* or *-iamo* endings to indicate soft sounds.

cominciare / to start, begin	*mangiare* / to eat
(io) comincio / I start	*(io) mangio* / I eat
(tu) cominci / you start	*(tu) mangi* / you eat
(lui/lei) comincia / he, she, it starts	*(lui/lei) mangia* / he, she, it eats
(noi) cominciamo / we start	*(noi) mangiamo* / we eat
(voi) cominciate / you start	*(voi) mangiate* / you eat
(loro) cominciano / they start	*(loro) mangiano* / they eat

The present indicative can be used with the preposition *da* (which in this case means both "since" and "for") to render the English present progressive tense.

I have been waiting	since	Monday
Aspetto	*da*	*lunedì*

She has been studying	for	four days
Studia	*da*	*quattro giorni*

Finally, you can use the present indicative to express an immediate future action.

> *Domani andiamo al teatro.* / Tomorrow we are going to the theater.
>
> *Domani parlo al professore.* / Tomorrow I will speak to the professor.

§8.2–2 Present Perfect

Il passato prossimo

The *present perfect tense* allows you to express simple actions completed at the present time. It is a compound tense, formed with the appropriate form of the auxiliary verb plus the past participle of the verb, in that order.

> *ho mangiato* / I have eaten, I ate, I did eat
>
> *ho* = auxiliary verb
> *mangiato* = past participle
>
> *sono andato* / I have gone
>
> *sono* = auxiliary verb
> *andato* = past participle

To form the past participle of regular verbs, do the following.

> Drop the infinitive ending.
>
> *parlare → parl-* / to speak
> *vendere → vend-* / to sell
> *dormire → dorm-* / to sleep
>
> Add the following endings.
>
> *parlato* / spoken
> *venduto* / sold
> *dormito* / slept

There are two auxiliary verbs: *avere* (to have) and *essere* to be. In the present perfect, these verbs are conjugated in the present indicative. Both are irregular.

	avere		*essere*	
io	ho	I have	sono	I am
tu	hai	you have	sei	you are
lui/lei	ha	he/she has, you have	è	he/she is, you are
noi	abbiamo	we have	siamo	we are
voi	avete	you have	siete	you are
loro	hanno	they have	sono	they are

Conjugations of verbs with *avere*

parlare → parlato

(io)	ho parlato / I have spoken, I spoke, I did speak
(tu)	hai parlato / you have spoken, you spoke, you did speak
(lui/lei)	ha parlato / he, she, you (pol.) has/have spoken, he, she, you (pol.) did speak
(noi)	abbiamo parlato / we have spoken, we spoke, we did speak
(voi)	avete parlato / you have spoken, you spoke, you did speak
(loro)	hanno parlato / they have spoken, they spoke, they did speak

vendere → venduto

(io)	ho venduto/ I have sold, I sold, I did sell
(tu)	hai venduto / you have sold, you sold, you did sell
(lui/lei)	ha venduto / he, she, you (pol.) has/have sold, he, she, you (pol.) sold, he, she, you (pol.) did sell
(noi)	abbiamo venduto / we have sold, we sold, we did sell
(voi)	avete venduto / you have sold, you sold, you did sell
(loro)	hanno venduto / they have sold, they sold, they did sell

dormire → *dormito*

(io)	*ho dormito* / I have slept, I slept, I did sleep
(tu)	*hai dormito* / you have slept, you slept, you did sleep
(lui/lei)	*ha dormito* / he, she, you (pol.) has/have slept, he, she, you (pol.) slept, he, she, you (pol.) did sleep
(noi)	*abbiamo dormito* / we have slept, we slept, we did sleep
(voi)	*avete dormito* / you have slept, you slept, you did sleep
(loro)	*hanno dormito* / they have slept, they slept, they did sleep

Examples

Maria ha venduto la sua macchina. / Mary sold her car.
Ieri ho parlato al signor Verdi. / Yesterday, I spoke to Mr. Verdi.
Loro hanno dormito troppo ieri. / They slept too much yesterday.
Ho già mangiato. / I have already eaten.

The past participle of such verbs agrees with the object pronouns *lo*, *la*, *li*, *le*, and *ne* (§7.3–2 and §7.5).

Hai mangiato le pesche? / Did you eat the peaches?

Sì, le ho mangiate. / Yes, I ate them.

Ne ho mangiate tre. / I ate three of them.

Conjugations of verbs with *essere*

The past participle of verbs conjugated with *essere* agrees in number and gender with the subject in the same way that an adjective does (see §6.2).

arrivare / to arrive → *arrivato*

(io)	*sono arrivato (-a)* / I have arrived, I arrived, I did arrive
(tu)	*sei arrivato (-a)* / you have arrived, you arrived, you did arrive
(lui/lei)	*è arrivato (-a)* / he, she, you (pol.) has/have arrived, he, she, you (pol.) arrived, he, she, you (pol.) did arrive
(noi)	*siamo arrivati (-e)* / we have arrived, we arrived, we did arrive
(voi)	*siete arrivati (-e)* / you have arrived, you arrived, you did arrive
(loro)	*sono arrivati (-e)* / they have arrived, they arrived, they did arrive

cadere / to fall → *caduto*

(io)	*sono caduto (-a)* / I have fallen, I fell, I did fall
(tu)	*sei caduto (-a)* / you have fallen, you fell, you did fall
(lui/lei)	*è caduto (-a)* / he, she, you (pol.) has/have fallen, he, she, you (pol.) fell, he, she, you (pol.) did fall
(noi)	*siamo caduti (-e)* / we have fallen, we fell, we did fall
(voi)	*siete caduti (-e)* / you have fallen, you fell, you did fall
(loro)	*sono caduti (-e)* / they have fallen, they fell, they did fall

partire / to leave → *partito*

(io)	*sono partito (-a)* / I have left, I left, I did leave
(tu)	*sei partito (-a)* / you have left, you left, you did leave
(lui/lei)	*è partito (-a)* / he, she, you (pol.) has/have left, he, she, you (pol.) left, he, she, you (pol.) did leave
(noi)	*siamo partiti (-e)* / we have left, we left, we did leave
(voi)	*siete partiti (-e)* / you have left, you left, you did leave
(loro)	*sono partiti (-e)* / they have left, they left, they did leave

Examples

Il nostro amico è arrivato ieri. / Our friend arrived yesterday.
Tua cugina è arrivata la settimana scorsa. / Your cousin (f.) arrived last week.
Quando siete caduti? / When did you (pl.) fall down?
Quando è partita, signora Verdi? / When did you leave, Mrs. Verdi?

Remember that third person forms also apply to the polite address. Choose the ending of the past participle according to the sex of the person you are addressing.

Signor Verdi, è caduto Lei? / Mr. Verdi, did you fall?
Signora Verdi, è caduta Lei? / Mrs. Verdi, did you fall?

Tip	When do you use *avere* or *essere*? The best learning strategy is to assume that most verbs are conjugated with *avere* (which is true!), and then memorize the verbs conjugated with *essere*. All the latter are intransitive (that is, they do not take a direct object)

Common Verbs Conjugated with *Essere* in Compound Tenses	
andare / to go	*nascere* / to be born
arrivare / to arrive	*partire* / to leave
cadere / to fall	*stare* / to stay
entrare / to enter	*sembrare* / to seem
essere / to be	*tornare* / to return
diventare / to become	*uscire* / to go out
morire / to die	*venire* / to come

Impersonal verbs are all conjugated with *essere*. These are verbs that have only third person forms.

> *durare* / to last
> *Lo spettacolo è durato tre ore.* / The showed lasted three hours.
> *costare* / to cost
> *Quanto sono costate le arance?* / How much did the oranges cost?

§8.2–3 Imperfect

> *L'imperfetto dell'indicativo*

The present perfect allows you, in essence, to refer to a finished past action. This is an action that you can visualize as having started and ended.

> *Ieri ho dormito due ore.* / Yesterday I slept two hours.

If, however, it is necessary to refer to an action that continued for an indefinite period of time, then the *imperfect* tense is called for.

> *Ieri, mentre io dormivo, tu guardavi la TV.* / Yesterday, while I was sleeping, you watched TV.

The *imperfect* is also used to refer to habitual or repeated actions in the past, and to describe the characteristics of people and things as they used to be.

> *Quando ero giovane, suonavo il pianoforte.* / When I was young, I used to play the piano.
> *Da giovane, Sara aveva i capelli biondi.* / As a youth, Sarah had (used to have) blonde hair.

To form the imperfect, drop the infinitive suffix and add the following endings.

Person	Endings		
	1st Conjugation = are	2nd Conjugation = ere	3rd Conjugation = ire
1st sing. (io)	-avo	-evo	-ivo
2nd sing. (tu)	-avi	-evi	-ivi
3rd sing. (lui/lei)	-ava	-eva	-iva
1st pl. (noi)	-avamo	-evamo	-ivamo
2nd pl. (voi)	-avate	-evate	-ivate
3rd pl. (loro)	-avano	-evano	-ivano

Conjugations

parlare → parl-

(io)	*parlavo* / I was speaking, I used to speak
(tu)	*parlavi* / you were speaking, you used to speak
(lui/lei)	*parlava* / he, she, you (pol.) was/were speaking, he, she, you (pol.) used to speak
(noi)	*parlavamo* / we were speaking, we used to speak
(voi)	*parlavate* / you were speaking, you used to speak
(loro)	*parlavano* / they were speaking, they used to speak

scrivere → scriv-

(io)	*scrivevo/*	I was writing, I used to write
(tu)	*scrivevi /*	you were writing, you used to write
(lui/lei)	*scriveva /*	he, she, you (pol.) was/were writing,
		he, she, you (pol.) used to write
(noi)	*scrivevamo /*	we were writing, we used to write
(voi)	*scrivevate /*	you were writing, you used to write
(loro)	*scrivevano /*	they were writing, they used to write

finire → fin-

(io)	*finivo /*	I was finishing, I used to finish
(tu)	*finivi /*	you were finishing, you used to finish
(lui/lei)	*finiva /*	he, she, you (pol.) was/were finishing,
		he, she, you (pol.) used to finish
(noi)	*finivamo /*	we were finishing, we used to finish
(voi)	*finivate /*	you were finishing, you used to finish
(loro)	*finivano /*	they were finishing, they used to finish

Examples

Mentre tu studiavi, tuo fratello suonava il violoncello. / While you
  were studying, your brother was playing the cello.
Da giovane, mio cugino scriveva ogni mese. / As a youth, my
  cousin used to write every month.
Quando andava a scuola, Maria studiava molto. / When she was
  going to school, Mary used to study a lot.

Tip

Be careful when you pronounce the third person
plural forms! The accent is placed on the first vowel
of the ending.

parlavano / they were speaking
    |
  stress

scrivevano / they were writing
    |
  stress

You might get confused when comparing English and Italian
past tense usage. This is because sometimes English uses a

perfect tense that is normally covered by the imperfect in Italian. But in such cases, English also uses the imperfect.

> *Mentre dormivo, tu guardavi la TV.* / While I slept *or* was sleeping, you watched *or* were watching TV.

You must therefore always look for clues among the other words in a sentence to determine whether the imperfect should or should not be used. Words such as *mentre* (while), *sempre* (always), *di solito* (usually), etc. generally entail the use of the imperfect.

§8.2–4 Past Absolute

> *Il passato remoto*

The *past absolute* covers many of the same uses as the present perfect (§8.2–2). Specifically, it allows you to talk about actions that occurred in the distant past.

To form the past absolute, drop the infinitive suffix and add the following endings.

Person	Endings		
	1st Conjugation = are	**2nd Conjugation = ere**	**3rd Conjugation = ire**
1st sing. (io)	*-ai*	*-ei (-etti)*	*-ii*
2nd sing. (tu)	*-asti*	*-esti*	*-isti*
3rd sing. (lui/lei)	*-ò*	*-è (-ette)*	*-ì*
1st pl. (noi)	*-ammo*	*-emmo*	*-immo*
2nd pl. (voi)	*-aste*	*-este*	*-iste*
3rd pl. (loro)	*-arono*	*-erono (-ettero)*	*-irono*

Conjugations

cantare /to sing → *cant-*

(io)	*cantai* / I sang	
(tu)	*cantasti* / you sang	
(lui/lei)	*cantò* / he, she, you (pol.) sang	
(noi)	*cantammo* / we sang	
(voi)	*cantaste* / you sang	
(loro)	*cantarono* / they sang	

vendere / to sell → *vend-*

(io)	*vendei (vendetti)* / I sold
(tu)	*vendesti* / you sold
(lui/lei)	*vendè (vendette)* / he, she, you (pol.) sold
(noi)	*vendemmo* / we sold
(voi)	*vendeste* / you sold
(loro)	*venderono (vendettero)* / they sold

finire / to finish → *fin-*

(io)	*finii* / I finished
(tu)	*finisti* / you finished
(lui/lei)	*finì* / he, she, you (pol.) finished
(noi)	*finimmo* / we finished
(voi)	*finiste* / you finished
(loro)	*finirono* / they finished

Examples

I miei genitori tornarono in Italia nel 1989. / My parents returned to Italy in 1989.

Marco Polo portò tanti tesori indietro. / Marco Polo brought back many treasures.

Dopo che vendè (vendette) la macchina, lui comprò una motocicletta. / After he sold the car, he bought a motorcycle.

Finirono quel lavoro tanto tempo fa. / They finished that job a long time ago.

The past absolute cannot be used with temporal adverbs such as *già* (already), *poco fa* (a little while ago), etc. which limit the action to the immediate past (occurring within less than twenty-four hours). Only the present perfect can be used in such cases.

Only Present Perfect Used

Alessandro è arrivato poco tempo fa. / Alexander arrived a little while ago.
Le ho telefonato. / I have already phoned her.

Outside this restriction, the past absolute can be used (judiciously) as an alternative to the present perfect.

Present Perfect	=	Past Absolute
Maria è arrivata in Italia nel 1994. / Mary arrived in Italy in 1994.		*Maria arrivò in Italia nel 1994.*
Ieri ti ho telefonato alle due. / Yesterday, I phoned you at two.		*Ieri ti telefonai alle due.*

The past absolute is, however, the only true "literary" past tense. It is used in particular in the narration of historical events.

Colombo arrivò nel Nuovo Mondo nel 1492. / Columbus arrived in the New World in 1492.
Mozart morì molto giovane. / Mozart died very young.

Whatever tense you decide to use, you must use either one consistently, especially with verbs in dependent clauses.

Quando sono arrivati, mi hanno chiamato. / When they arrived, they called me.
     | |
   present   present
   perfect   perfect

Quando arrivarono, mi chiamarono. / When they arrived, they called me.
     | |
   past   past
   absolute   absolute

§8.2–5 Pluperfect

> *Il trapassato prossimo*

The pluperfect is a compound tense. As such, it is conjugated with an auxiliary verb, either *avere* or *essere*, and the past participle of the verb. (Review §8.2–2 for the details regarding compound tenses).

It is a formed with the imperfect of the auxiliary verb plus the past participle of the verb, in that order.

avevo mangiato / I had eaten

avevo = auxiliary verb in the imperfect
mangiato = past participle

ero andato / I had gone

ero = auxiliary verb in the imperfect
andato = part participle

In the imperfect, the auxiliary verbs are conjugated as follows:

	avere		*essere*	
io	*avevo*	I used to have	*ero*	I used to be
tu	*avevi*	you used have	*eri*	you used to be
lui/lei	*aveva*	he/she has, you used to have	*era*	he/she, you used to be
noi	*avevamo*	we used to have	*eravamo*	we used to be
voi	*avevate*	you used to have	*eravate*	you used to be
loro	*avevano*	they used to have	*erano*	they used to be

Conjugations of verbs with *avere*

parlare → *parlato*

(io)	*avevo parlato* / I had spoken
(tu)	*avevi parlato* / you had spoken
(lui/lei)	*aveva parlato* / he, she, you (pol.) had spoken
(noi)	*avevamo parlato* / we had spoken
(voi)	*avevate parlato* / you had spoken
(loro)	*avevano parlato* / they had spoken

vendere → *venduto*

(io)	*avevo venduto*/ I had sold
(tu)	*avevi venduto* / you had sold
(lui/lei)	*aveva venduto* / he, she, you (pol.) had sold
(noi)	*avevamo venduto* / we had sold
(voi)	*avevate venduto* / you had sold
(loro)	*avevano venduto* / they had sold

dormire → *dormito*

(io)	*avevo dormito* / I had slept
(tu)	*avevi dormito* / you had slept
(lui/lei)	*aveva dormito* / he, she, you (pol.) had slept
(noi)	*avevamo dormito* / we had slept
(voi)	*avevate dormito* / you had slept
(loro)	*avevano dormito* / they had slept

Conjugations of verbs with *essere*

arrivare / to arrive → *arrivato*

(io)	*ero arrivato (-a)* / I had arrived
(tu)	*eri arrivato (-a)* / you had arrived
(lui/lei)	*era arrivato (-a)* / he, she, you (pol.) had arrived
(noi)	*eravamo arrivati (-e)* / we had arrived
(voi)	*eravate arrivati (-e)* / you had arrived
(loro)	*erano arrivati (-e)* / they had arrived

cadere / to fall → *caduto*

(io)	*ero caduto (-a)*/ I had fallen
(tu)	*eri caduto (-a)*/ you had fallen
(lui/lei)	*era caduto (-a)* / he, she, you (pol.) had fallen
(noi)	*eravamo caduti (-e)* / we had fallen
(voi)	*eravate caduti (-e)* / you had fallen
(loro)	*erano caduti (-e)* / they had fallen

partire / to leave → *partito*

(io)	*ero partito (-a)* / I had left
(tu)	*eri partito (-a)* / you had left
(lui/lei)	*era partito (-a)* / he, she, you (pol.) had left
(noi)	*eravamo partiti (-e)* / we had left
(voi)	*eravate partiti (-e)* / you had left
(loro)	*erano partiti (-e)* / they had left

The *pluperfect* tense (literally, "more than perfect" or "more than past") allows you to express an action that occurred *before* a simple past action (as expressed by the present perfect, the imperfect, or the past absolute).

Dopo che era arrivata, mi ha telefonato. / After she had arrived, she phoned me.

    | |
  pluperfect   present
(occurred before phoning) perfect

Lui mi ha detto che le aveva già parlato. / He told me that he had already talked to her.

    | |
  present   pluperfect
  perfect   *(occurred before)*

> **Tip**
>
> Essentially, this tense corresponds to the English pluperfect ("had + past participle"). But be careful! Sometimes the pluperfect is only implied in English colloquial usage.
>
> *Sono andati in Italia dopo che avevano finito gli esami.* / They went to Italy after they finished (= had finished) their exams.

§8.2–6 Simple Future

> *Il futuro semplice*

The *simple future*, as its name implies, allows you to express an action that will occur in the future. To form the simple future, do the following.

Drop the final -e of the infinitives of all three conjugations, changing the -ar of first conjugation verbs to -er simultaneously.

parlare → *parler-*
scrivere → *scriver-*
finire → *finir-*

Add on the following endings.

Person	Endings for All Conjugations
1st sing. (io)	*-ò*
2nd sing. (tu)	*-ai*
3rd sing. (lui/lei)	*-à*
1st pl. (noi)	*-emo*
2nd pl. (voi)	*-ete*
3rd pl. (loro)	*-anno*

Conjugations

parlare → *parl-*

(io)	*parlerò* / I will speak
(tu)	*parlerai* / you will speak
(lui/lei)	*parlerà* / he, she, you (pol.) will speak
(noi)	*parleremo* / we will speak
(voi)	*parlerete* / you will speak
(loro)	*parleranno* / they will speak

scrivere → *scriver-*

(io)	*scriverò* / I will write
(tu)	*scriverai* / you will write
(lui/lei)	*scriverà* / he, she, you (pol.) will write
(noi)	*scriveremo* / we will write
(voi)	*scriverete* / you will write
(loro)	*scriveranno* / they will write

finire → finir-

(io)	*finirò* / I will finish
(tu)	*finirai* / you will finish
(lui/lei)	*finirà* / he, she, you (pol.) will finish
(noi)	*finiremo* / we will finish
(voi)	*finirete* / you will finish
(loro)	*finiranno* / they will finish

Recall that the hard *c* and hard *g* sounds are indicated in first conjugation verbs by adding an *h* before endings beginning with an *-e* or an *-i* (see §8.2–1). This applies to the future tense too.

cercare / to search for →
  cercher-

(io) cercherò / I will search
(tu) cercherai / you will search
(lui/lei) cercherà / he, she,
  you (pol.) will search
(noi) cercheremo / we will search
(voi) cercherete / you will search
(loro) cercheranno /
  they will search

pagare / to pay (for) →
  pagher-

(io) pagherò / I will pay
(tu) pagherai / you will pay
(lui/lei) pagherà / he, she,
  you (pol.) will pay
(noi) pagheremo / we will pay
(voi) pagherete / you will pay
(loro) pagheranno /
  they will pay

And if the verb ends in *-ciare* or *-giare*, then you no longer need the *-i* because of the change of the *-ar* ending to *-er* throughout the conjugation.

cominciare / to start → cominicer-

(io) comincerò / I will start
(tu) comincerai / you will start
(lui/lei) comincerà /
  he, she, you (pol.) will start
(noi) cominceremo / we will start
(voi) comincerete / you will start
(loro) cominceranno /
  they will start

mangiare / to eat → manger-

(io) mangerò / I will eat
(tu) mangerai / you will eat
(lui/lei) mangerà / he, she,
  you (pol.) will eat
(noi) mangeremo / we will eat
(voi) mangerete / you will eat
(loro) mangeranno /
  they will eat

The future tense corresponds, generally, to the English future—"I will go," "you will write," etc. It also conveys the idea expressed in English with "going to":

Manderò un e-mail al mio amico domani. / I will send an e-mail to my friend tomorrow *or* I'm going to send an e-mail to my friend tomorrow.

Partiranno tra un mese. / They will leave in a month. *or* They are going to leave in a month.

The Italian future is also used to convey probability.

Sai quanto costa quell'orologio? / Do you know how much that watch costs?

Costerà mille dollari americani. / It probably costs 1000 American dollars.

Qualcuno bussa alla porta. / Someone is knocking at the door.

A quest'ora sarà tua sorella. / At this hour it is probably your sister.

§8.2–7 Future Perfect

> *Il futuro anteriore/perfetto*

Like the present perfect (see §8.2–2) and the pluperfect (see §8.2–5), the future perfect is a compound tense.

It is a formed with the future of the auxiliary verb plus the past participle of the verb, in that order.

avrò mangiato / I will have eaten

avrò = auxiliary verb in the future
mangiato = past participle

sarò andato / I will have gone

sarò = auxiliary verb in the future
andato = past participle

In the future, the auxiliary verbs are conjugated as follows:

	avere		*essere*	
io	avrò	I will have	sarò	I will be
tu	avrai	you will have	sarai	you will be
lui/lei	avrà	he/she you, will have	sarà	he/she you will be
noi	avremo	we will have	saremo	we will be
voi	avrete	you will have	sarete	you will be
loro	avranno	they will have	saranno	they will be

Conjugations of verbs with *avere*

parlare → *parlato*

(io)	avrò parlato / I will have spoken
(tu)	avrai parlato / you will have spoken
(lui/lei)	avrà parlato / he, she, you (pol.) will have spoken
(noi)	avremo parlato / we will have spoken
(voi)	avrete parlato / you will have spoken
(loro)	avranno parlato / they will have spoken

vendere → *venduto*

(io)	avrò venduto / I will have sold
(tu)	avrai venduto / you will have sold
(lui/lei)	avrà venduto / he, she, you (pol.) will have sold
(noi)	avremo venduto / we will have sold
(voi)	avrete venduto / you will have sold
(loro)	avranno venduto / they will have sold

dormire → *dormito*

(io)	avrò dormito / I will have slept
(tu)	avrai dormito / you will have slept
(lui/lei)	avrà dormito / he, she, you (pol.) will have slept
(noi)	avremo dormito / we will have slept
(voi)	avrete dormito / you will have slept
(loro)	avranno dormito / they will have slept

Conjugations of verbs with *essere*

arrivare / to arrive → *arrivato*

(io)	*sarò arrivato (-a)* / I will have arrived
(tu)	*sarai arrivato (-a)* / you will have arrived
(lui/lei)	*sarà arrivato (-a)* / he, she, you (pol.) will have arrived
(noi)	*saremo arrivati (-e)* / we will have arrived
(voi)	*sarete arrivati (-e)* / you will have arrived
(loro)	*saranno arrivati (-e)* / they will have arrived

cadere / to fall → *caduto*

(io)	*sarò caduto (-a)* / I will have fallen
(tu)	*sarai caduto (-a)* / you will have fallen
(lui/lei)	*sarà caduto (-a)* / he, she, you (pol.) will have fallen
(noi)	*saremo caduti (-e)* / we will have fallen
(voi)	*sarete caduti (-e)* / you will have fallen
(loro)	*saranno caduti (-e)* / they will have fallen

partire / to leave → *partito*

(io)	*sarò partito (-a)* / I will have left
(tu)	*sarai partito (-a)* / you will have left
(lui/lei)	*sarà partito (-a)* / he, she, you (pol.) will have left
(noi)	*saremo partiti (-e)* / we will have left
(voi)	*sarete partiti (-e)* / you will have left
(loro)	*saranno partiti (-e)* / they will have left

Generally, this tense corresponds to the English future perfect. It is used to refer to actions that occurred before simple future actions.

Andremo al cinema, appena avrai finito di lavorare. / We will go to the movies, as soon as you (will) have finished work.

future

future
perfect
(occurs before going)

However, in conversational Italian, the simple future can often be used instead.

Andremo al cinema, appena finirai di lavorare. / We will go to the movies, as soon as you finish work.

Like the simple future, the future perfect can also be used to convey probability (see §8.2–6).

> *Quanto sarà costata quella macchina?* / How much did that car probably cost?
> *Sarà costata un occhio della testa.* / It must have cost an arm and a leg.
> *A che ora ha telefonato?* / At what time did he phone?
> *Avrà telefonato alle sei.* / He must have phoned at six.

§8.3 THE IMPERATIVE

The imperative allows you to give commands and advice.

To form the imperative, drop the infinitive ending of the verb, and then add the following endings to the stem according to the conjugation.

Person	Endings		
	1st Conjugation = are	2nd Conjugation = ere	3rd Conjugation = ire
1st sing. (io)	-	-	-
2nd sing. (tu)	*-a*	*-i*	*-i / -isci*
3rd sing. (lui/lei)	*-i*	*-a*	*-a / -isca*
1st pl. (noi)	*-iamo*	*-iamo*	*-iamo / -iamo*
2nd pl. (voi)	*-ate*	*-ete*	*-ite / -ite*
3rd pl. (loro)	*-ino*	*-ano*	*-ano/ -iscano*

Conjugations

aspettare / to wait → *aspett-*

(tu)	aspetta / wait
(Lei)	aspetti / wait
(noi)	aspettiamo / let's wait
(voi)	aspettate / wait
(Loro)	aspettino / wait

scrivere / to write → *scriv-*

(tu)	scrivi / write
(Lei)	scriva / write
(noi)	scriviamo / let's write
(voi)	scrivete / write
(Loro)	scrivano / write

aprire / to open → *apr-*

(tu)	apri / open
(Lei)	apra / open
(noi)	apriamo / let's open
(voi)	aprite / open
(Loro)	aprano / open

finire → *fin-*

(tu)	finisci / finish
(Lei)	finisca / finish
(noi)	finiamo / let's finish
(voi)	finite / finish
(Loro)	finiscano / finish

> **Tip**
>
> The distinction in conjugation pattern between *aprire*-type verbs and *finire*-type verbs applies only to the present indicative (§8.2–1), the imperative (this section), and the present subjunctive (§8.5–1)

Examples

Alessandro, aspetta qui! / Alexander, wait here!

Signora Binni, scriva il Suo nome qui! / Mrs. Binni, write your name here!

Studenti, aprite i vostri libri a pagina 4! / Students, open your books at page 4!

Signora Binni e Signor Binni, aspettate qui! / Mrs. Binni and Mr. Binni, wait here!

Signore, per favore finisca di lamentarsi! / Sir, please stop (finish) complaining!

Recall (§7.3–1 and §7.3–2) that the *voi* forms are used as the plural forms of both *tu* (familiar) and *Lei* (polite) singular forms. The *Loro* forms are rarely used:

Tu form (sing.)
Bambina, mangia la mela! / Little girl, eat the apple!

Voi form (pl.)
Bambine, mangiate la mela! / Little girls, eat the apple!

Lei form (sing.)
Signora, mangi la mela! / Madam, eat the apple!

Voi form (sing.)
Signore, mangiate la mela! / Ladies, eat the apple!

Loro form (pl.)
Signore, mangino la mela! / Ladies, eat the apple!

Recall that the hard *c* and hard *g* sounds in -*care* and -*gare* verbs are indicated by adding an *h* before endings beginning with an -*e* or an -*i* (see §8.2–1). This applies to the imperative tense as well.

cercare / to search for	*pagare* / to pay (for)
(tu) cerca / search	*(tu) paga* / pay
(Lei) cerchi / search	*(Lei) paghi* / pay
(noi) cerchiamo / let's search	*(noi) paghiamo* / let's pay
(voi) cercate / search	*(voi) pagate* / pay
(Loro) cerchino / search	*(Loro) paghino* / pay

And if the verb ends in *-ciare* or *-giare*, then you do not repeat the *-i* before an ending beginning with *-i*

cominciare / to start	*mangiare* / to eat
(tu) comincia / start	*(tu) mangia* / eat
(Lei) cominci / start	*(Lei) mangi* / eat
(noi) cominciamo / let's start	*(noi) mangiamo* / let's eat
(voi) cominciate / start	*(voi) mangiate* / eat
(loro) comincino / start	*(loro) mangino* / eat

Examples

Signor Dini, cerchi i Suoi occhiali! / Mr. Dini, look for your glasses!
Paghiamo il conto! / Let's pay the bill!
Signori, paghino il conto! / Gentlemen, pay the bill!
Signora, cominci per favore! / Madam, please begin!
E ora, mangiamo! / And now, let's eat!

To form the negative imperative, add *non* in the usual way (§2.2–2). But you must make one adjustment—the second person singular form must be changed to the infinitive of the verb.

Examples

Affirmative	**Negative**
2nd Person Singular	
Aspetta! / Wait!	*Non aspettare!* / Don't wait!
Scrivi! / Write!	*Non scrivere!* / Don't write!
Finisci! / Finish!	*Non finire!* / Don't finish!
Other Persons	
Aspetti! / Wait! (pol.)	*Non aspetti!* / Don't wait!
Scriviamo! / Let's write!	*Non scriviamo!* / Let's not write!
Finite! / Finish!	*Non finite!* / Don't finish!

The object pronouns are attached to the familiar forms only.
They are not attached to the polite *Lei* and *Loro* forms.

Examples

Polite Forms
Signor Binni, mi telefoni! / Mr. Binni, phone me!
Signora Dini, gliela scriva! / Mrs. Dini, write it to him!
Signori, ce li mandino! / Gentlemen, send them to us!

Other Forms
Sara, telefonami! / Sarah, phone me!
Alessandro, scrivigliela! / Alexander, write it to him!
Amici, mandateceli! / Friends, send them to us!

The second person singular imperative forms of *dare* (to give), *dire* (to say), *fare* (to do, make), *andare* (to go), and *stare* (to stay) are written with an apostrophe (see *Verb Charts* section at the back of this book).

Da' la penna a me! / Give the pen to me!
Di' la verità! / Tell the truth!
Fa' qualcosa! / Do something!
Va' via! / Go away!
Sta' qui! / Stay here!

When attaching pronouns to these forms, you must double the first letter (sound) of the pronoun:

Dammi la penna! / Give me the pen!
Dilla! / Tell it (*la verità*)!
Fallo! / Do it!

There is, of course, no double *gl*:

Digli la verità! / Tell him the truth.
Faglielo! / Do it for him!

With the second person singular negative infinitive form (see above), you can either attach the pronouns to the infinitive or else put them before. Notice that the final *-e* of the infinitive is dropped when attaching pronouns.

Examples

Affirmative	Negative
Mangialo! / Eat it!	*Non mangiarlo!* or *Non lo mangiare!* / Don't eat it!

Mandamela! /   *Non mandarmela! or Non me la mandare! /*
Send it to me!   Don't send it to me!

§8.4 THE CONDITIONAL TENSES

> *Il condizionale*

The conditional mood allows you to express a condition: "I *would* go if . . ."; "We *would* do it, but . . ."; etc.

§8.4–1 Present

> *Il condizionale presente*

To form the present conditional, do the following.

As you did for the simple future (review §8.2–6), drop the final *-e* of the infinitives of all three conjugations, changing the *-ar* of first conjugation verbs to *-er* simultaneously:

parlare → parler-
scrivere → scriver-
finire → finir-

Add on the following endings.

Person	Endings for All Conjugations
1st sing. (io)	*-ei*
2nd sing. (tu)	*-esti*
3rd sing. (lui/lei)	*-ebbe*
1st pl. (noi)	*-emmo*
2nd pl. (voi)	*-este*
3rd pl. (loro)	*-ebbero*

Conjugations

parlare → *parl-*

(io)	*parlerei* / I would speak
(tu)	*parleresti* / you would speak
(lui/lei)	*parlerebbe* / he, she, you (pol.) would speak
(noi)	*parleremmo* / we would speak
(voi)	*parlereste* / you would speak
(loro)	*parlerebbero* / they would speak

scrivere → *scriver-*

(io)	*scriverei* / I would write
(tu)	*scriveresti* / you would write
(lui/lei)	*scriverebbe* / he, she, you (pol.) would write
(noi)	*scriveremmo* / we would write
(voi)	*scrivereste* / you would write
(loro)	*scriverebbero* / they would write

finire → *finir-*

(io)	*finirei* / I would finish
(tu)	*finiresti* / you would finish
(lui/lei)	*finirebbe* / he, she, you (pol.) would finish
(noi)	*finiremmo* / we would finish
(voi)	*finireste* / you would finish
(loro)	*finirebbero* / they would finish

Recall that the hard *c* and hard *g* sounds in -*care* and -*gare* verbs are indicated by adding an *h* before endings beginning with an -*e* or an -*i* (see §8.2–6). This applies to the conditional tense too.

cercare / to search for → cercher-	*pagare* / to pay (for) → pagher-
(io) cercherei / I would search	*(io) pagherei* / I would pay
(tu) cercheresti / you would search	*(tu) pagheresti* / you would pay
(lui/lei) cercherebbe / he, she, you (pol.) would search	*(lui/lei) pagherebbe* / he, she, you (pol.) would pay
(noi) cercheremmo / we would search	*(noi) pagheremmo* / we would pay
(voi) cerchereste / you would search	*(voi) paghereste* / you would pay

(loro) cercherebbero / they would search	*(loro)* pagherebbero / they would pay

And if the verb ends in *-ciare* or *-giare*, then you no longer need the *-i*.

cominciare / to start → *comincer-*	*mangiare* / to eat → *manger-*
(io) comincerei / I would start	*(io)* mangerei / I would eat
(tu) cominceresti / you would start	*(tu)* mangeresti / you would eat
(lui/lei) comincerebbe / he, she, you (pol.) would start	*(lui/lei)* mangerebbe / he, she, you (pol.) would eat
(noi) cominceremmo / we would start	*(noi)* mangeremmo / we would eat
(voi) comincereste / you would start	*(voi)* mangereste / you would eat
(loro) comincerebbero / they would start	*(loro)* mangerebbero / they would eat

The conditional tense corresponds, generally, to the English conditional—"I would go," "you would write," etc.

Examples

Pagherei il conto, ma non ho soldi. / I would pay the bill, but I have no money.

Comprerebbero quella casa nuova, ma non hanno ancora venduto la vecchia casa. / They would buy that new home, but they haven't yet sold the old house.

In addition, it is used:

To express a polite request
Potrei parlare? / May I speak?
Mi darebbe quella lì? / Could you give me that one?

To quote someone else's opinion
Secondo lui, quella ragazza sarebbe spagnola. /
    According to him, that girl is (probably) Spanish.
Secondo loro, l'Italia sarebbe il miglior paese del mondo. /
    In their opinion, Italy is the best country in the world.

§8.4–2 Past

> *Il condizionale perfetto*

The past conditional is a compound tense (§8.2–2). It is formed with the conditional of the auxiliary verb plus the past participle of the verb, in that order.

> *avrei mangiato* / I would have eaten
> *avrei* = auxiliary verb in the conditional
> *mangiato* = past participle
>
> *sarei andato* / I would have gone
> *sarei* = auxiliary verb in the conditional
> *andato* = past participle

In the conditional, the auxiliary verbs are conjugated as follows:

	avere		*essere*	
io	avrei	I will have	sarei	I will be
tu	avresti	you will have	saresti	you will be
lui/lei	avrebbe	he/she, you will have	sarebbe	he/she, you will be
noi	avremmo	we will have	saremmo	we will be
voi	avreste	you will have	sareste	you will be
loro	avrebbero	they will have	sarebbero	they will be

Conjugations of verbs with *avere*

parlare / to speak → *parlato*

(io)	*avrei parlato* / I will have spoken
(tu)	*avresti parlato* / you will have spoken
(lui/lei)	*avrebbe parlato* / he, she, you (pol.) will have spoken
(noi)	*avremmo parlato* / we will have spoken

| *(voi)* | avreste parlato / you will have spoken |
| *(loro)* | avrebbero parlato / they will have spoken |

vendere / to sell → *venduto*

(io)	avrei venduto/ I will have sold
(tu)	avresti venduto / you will have sold
(lui/lei)	avrebbe venduto / he, she, you (pol.) will have sold
(noi)	avremmo venduto / we will have sold
(voi)	avreste venduto / you will have sold
(loro)	avrebbero venduto / they will have sold

dormire / to sleep → *dormito*

(io)	avrei dormito / I will have slept
(tu)	avresti dormito / you will have slept
(lui/lei)	avrebbe dormito / he, she, you (pol.) will have slept
(noi)	avremmo dormito / we will have slept
(voi)	avreste dormito / you will have slept
(loro)	avrebbero dormito / they will have slept

Conjugations of verbs with *essere*

arrivare / to arrive → *arrivato*

(io)	sarei arrivato (-a) / I will have arrived
(tu)	saresti arrivato (-a) / you will have arrived
(lui/lei)	sarebbe arrivato (-a) / he, she, you (pol.) will have arrived
(noi)	saremmo arrivati (-e) / we will have arrived
(voi)	sareste arrivati (-e) / you will have arrived
(loro)	sarebbero arrivati (-e) / they will have arrived

cadere / to fall → *caduto*

(io)	sarei caduto (-a)/ I will have fallen
(tu)	saresti caduto (-a)/ you will have fallen
(lui/lei)	sarebbe caduto (-a) / he, she, you (pol.) will have fallen
(noi)	saremmo caduti (-e) / we will have fallen
(voi)	sareste caduti (-e) / you will have fallen
(loro)	sarebbero caduti (-e) / they will have fallen

partire / to leave → *partito*

(io)	sarei partito (-a) / I will have left
(tu)	saresti partito (-a) / you will have left
(lui/lei)	sarebbe partito (-a) / he, she, you (pol.) will have left

(noi)	*saremmo partiti (-e)* / we will have left	
(voi)	*sareste partiti (-e)* / you will have left	
(loro)	*sarebbero partiti (-e)* / they will have left	

Generally, this tense corresponds to the English past conditional ("I would have . . ."; "You would have . . ."; etc.). It is used to refer to actions that occurred before simple future actions.

> *Mi ha detto che sarebbe venuto.* / He told me that he would (would have) come.
> *Sapeva che io avrei capito.* / He knew I would have understood.

§8.5 THE SUBJUNCTIVE TENSES

> *Il congiuntivo*

The subjunctive mood allows you to express a point of view, fear, doubt, hope, possibility—that is, anything that is not a fact. In a way, the subjunctive is a counterpart to the indicative, the mood that allows you to convey facts and information.

§8.5–1 Present

> *Il congiuntivo presente*

To form the present indicative, do the following:

> Drop the infinitive ending of the verb.
> *parlare → parl-* / to speak
> *scrivere → scriv-* / to write
> *aprire → apr-* / to open
> *capire → cap-* / to understand

> Add the following endings to the stem according to the conjugation.

Person	Endings		
	1st Conjugation = are	**2nd Conjugation** = ere	**3rd Conjugation** = ire
1st sing. (io)	-i	-a	-a / -isca
2nd sing. (tu)	-i	-a	-a / -isca
3rd sing. (lui/lei)	-i	-a	-a / -isca
1st pl. (noi)	-iamo	-iamo	-iamo / -iamo
2nd pl. (voi)	-iate	-iate	-iate / -iate
3rd pl. (loro)	-ino	-ano	-ano / -iscano

Conjugations

parlare → parl-

(io)	parli / I speak, I am speaking, I do speak
(tu)	parli / you speak, you are speaking, you do speak
(lui/lei)	parli / he, she, you (pol.) speak(s), he, she, you (pol.) is/ are speaking, he, she, you (pol.) does/do speak
(noi)	parliamo / we speak, we are speaking, we do speak
(voi)	parliate / you speak, you are speaking, you do speak
(loro)	parlino / they speak, they are speaking, they do speak

scrivere → scriv-

(io)	scriva / I write, I am writing, I do write
(tu)	scriva / you write, you are writing, you do write
(lui/lei)	scriva / he, she, you (pol.) write(s), he, she, you (pol.) is/ are writing, he, she, you (pol.) does/do write
(noi)	scriviamo / we write, we are writing, we do write
(voi)	scriviate / you write, you are writing, you do write
(loro)	scrivano / they write, they are writing, they do write

aprire → *apr-*

(io)	*apra*	/ I open, I am opening, I do open
(tu)	*apra*	/ you open, you are opening, you do open
(lui/lei)	*apra*	/ he, she, you (pol.) open(s), he, she, you (pol.) is (are) opening, he, she, you (pol.) does/do open
(noi)	*apriamo*	/ we open, we are opening, we do open
(voi)	*apriate*	/ you open, you are opening, you do open
(loro)	*aprano*	/ they open, they are opening, they do open

capire → *cap-*

(io)	*capisca*	/ I understand, I do understand
(tu)	*capisca*	/ you understand, you do understand
(lui/lei)	*capisca*	/ he, she, you (pol.) understand(s), he, she, you (pol.) does/do understand
(noi)	*capiamo*	/ we understand, we are understanding, we do understand
(voi)	*capiate*	/ you understand, you are understanding, you do understand
(loro)	*capiscano*	/ they understand, they are understanding, they do understand

---

Because the endings are often the same, you will need to use the subject pronouns much more frequently with the subjunctive.

È necessario che tu finisca quel lavoro. / It is important that you finish that job.

È necessario che lui finisca quel lavoro. / It is important that he finish that job.

As with the present indicative (§8.2–1) and imperative you will have to learn whether a given third conjugation verb follows the pattern of *aprire* or *capire*. A good dictionary will provide this kind of information.

Tip	Be careful when you pronounce the third person plural forms! The accent is *not* placed on the ending.

parlino / they speak   *scrivano* / they write
    | |
stress   stress

Again, if a verb ends in -*care* or -*gare*, then you indicate the hard sound by adding an *h* before the endings starting with -*i*. In this case, the *h* is used throughout the conjugation pattern:

cercare / to search for

(io) cerchi / I search
(tu) cerchi / you search
(lui/lei) cerchi / he, she, you (pol.) searches/search
(noi) cerchiamo / we search
(voi) cerchiate / you search
(loro) cerchino / they search

pagare / to pay (for)

(io) paghi / I pay
(tu) paghi / you pay
(lui/lei) paghi / he, she, you (pol.) pays/pay
(noi) paghiamo / we pay
(voi) paghiate / you pay
(loro) paghino / they pay

If a first conjugation verb ends in -*ciare* or -*giare*, then you no longer need the -*i* of the infinitive suffix:

cominciare / to start, begin

(io) cominci / I start
(tu) cominci / you start
(lui/lei) cominci / he, she, you (pol.) starts/start
(noi) cominciamo / we start
(voi) cominciate / you start
(loro) comincino / they start

mangiare / to eat

(io) mangi / I eat
(tu) mangi / you eat
(lui/lei) mangi / he, she, you (pol.) eats/eat
(noi) mangiamo / we eat
(voi) mangiate / you eat
(loro) mangino / they eat

Tip

> The subjunctive is used in subordinate clauses, generally introduced by *che*. So, when expressing something that is a doubt, an opinion, etc. with a verb in the main clause (the verb *to the left* of *che*), then put the verb in the subordinate clause (the verb *to the right* of *che*) in the subjunctive.
>
> *Spero che loro parlino italiano.* / I hope that they speak Italian.
> | hope   subjunctive

Keep in mind that not all verbs in subordinate clauses (those after *che*) are necessarily to be put in the subjunctive—only those connected to a main clause verb that expresses a "non-fact" (opinion, fear, supposition, anticipation, wish, hope, doubt, etc.).

Indicative
Sa che è la verità. / He (she) knows it is the truth.
È certo che paga lui. / It is certain that he will pay.

Subjunctive
Pensa che sia la verità. / He (she) thinks it is the truth.
È improbabile che paghi lui. / It is improbable that he will pay.

Tip

> The best way to learn which main clause verbs require the subjunctive is to memorize the most commonly used ones. Here are a few of them.
>
> *credere* / to believe   *pensare* / to think
> *desiderare* / to desire   *sembrare* / to seem
> *dubitare* / to doubt   *sperare* / to hope
> *immaginare* / to imagine   *volere* / to want

Examples

> *Crede che loro arrivino stasera.* / He thinks (that) they are arriving tonight.
>
> *Immagino che lei capisca tutto.* / I imagine (that) she understands everything.
>
> *Dubitano che voi finiate in tempo.* / They doubt that you will finish in time.

Impersonal verbs and expressions also require that the subordinate clause verb be in the subjunctive.

> *È probabile che lui non ti riconosca più.* / It's probable that he will not recognize you anymore.
>
> *Bisogna che voi studiate di più.* / It is necessary that you study more.

Superlative expressions (review §6.5) also require the subjunctive.

> *Lei è la persona più intelligente che io conosca.* / She is the most intelligent person I know.
>
> *Tu sei la persona meno elegante che io conosca.* / You are the least elegant person I know.

Certain conjunctions and indefinite structures also require the subjunctive.

> *Dovunque tu vada, io ti seguirò.* / Wherever you go, I will follow you.
>
> *Benché piova, esco lo stesso.* / Although it is raining, I'm going out just the same.

The most commonly used structures with this feature are:

chiunque / whoever	*dovunque* / wherever
qualsiasi cosa / whatever	*qualunque cosa* / whichever
affinché / so that	*benché* / although
sebbene / although	*come se* / as if
senza che / without	*nel caso che* / in the event that
prima che / before	*nonostante che* / despite
purché / provided that	*perché* / so that

Finally, the subjunctive is used in "wish" or "exhortation" expressions.

Examples

Che scriva lui! / Let him write!
Che piova, se vuole! / Let it rain, if it wants to!
Che Dio ce la mandi buona! / God help us!

§8.5–2 Past

> *Il congiuntivo
> perfetto/passato*

Like the present perfect (see §8.2–2), the past subjunctive is a compound tense.

It is a formed with the present subjunctive of the auxiliary verb plus the past participle of the verb, in that order.

abbia mangiato / I have eaten
abbia = auxiliary verb in the present subjunctive
mangiato = past participle

sia andato / I have gone
sia = auxiliary verb in the present subjunctive
andato = past participle

In the present subjunctive, the auxiliary verbs are conjugated as follows:

	avere		*essere*	
io	*abbia*	I have	*sia*	I am
tu	*abbia*	you have	*sia*	you are
lui/lei	*abbia*	he/she, you have	*sia*	he/she, you is
noi	*abbiamo*	we have	*siamo*	we are
voi	*abbia*	you have	*siate*	you are
loro	*abbiano*	they have	*siano*	they are

Conjugations of verbs with *avere*

parlare / to speak → *parlato*

(io)	*abbia parlato* / I have spoken	
(tu)	*abbia parlato* / you have spoken	
(lui/lei)	*abbia parlato* / he, she, you (pol.) have spoken	
(noi)	*abbiamo parlato* / we have spoken	
(voi)	*abbiate parlato* / you have spoken	
(loro)	*abbiano parlato* / they have spoken	

vendere / to sell → *venduto*

(io)	*abbia venduto* / I have sold	
(tu)	*abbia venduto* / you have sold	
(lui/lei)	*abbia venduto* / he, she, you (pol.) has/have sold	
(noi)	*abbiamo venduto* / we have sold	
(voi)	*abbiate venduto* / you have sold	
(loro)	*abbiano venduto* / they have sold	

dormire / to sleep → *dormito*

(io)	*abbia dormito* / I have slept	
(tu)	*abbia dormito* / you have slept	
(lui/lei)	*abbia dormito* / he, she, you (pol.) have slept	
(noi)	*abbiamo dormito* / we have slept	
(voi)	*abbiate dormito* / you have slept	
(loro)	*abbiano dormito* / they have slept	

Conjugations of verbs with *essere*

arrivare / to arrive → *arrivato*

(io)	*sia arrivato (-a)* / I have arrived	
(tu)	*sia arrivato (-a)* / you have arrived	
(lui/lei)	*sia arrivato (-a)* / he, she, you (pol.) have arrived	
(noi)	*siamo arrivati (-e)* / we have arrived	
(voi)	*siate arrivati (-e)* / you have arrived	
(loro)	*siano arrivati (-e)* / they have arrived	

cadere / to fall → *caduto*

(io)	*sia caduto (-a)* / I have fallen	
(tu)	*sia caduto (-a)* / you have fallen	

(lui/lei)	*sia caduto (-a)* / he, she, you (pol.) have fallen
(noi)	*siamo caduti (-e)* / we have fallen
(voi)	*siate caduti (-e)* / you have fallen
(loro)	*siano caduti (-e)* / they have fallen

partire / to leave → *partito*

(io)	*sia partito (-a)* / I have left
(tu)	*sia partito (-a)* / you have left
(lui/lei)	*sia partito (-a)* / he, she, you (pol.) have left
(noi)	*siamo partiti (-e)* / we have left
(voi)	*siate partiti (-e)* / you have left
(loro)	*siano partiti (-e)* / they have left

The past subjunctive corresponds to the present perfect in temporal usage (see §8.2–2). Essentially, it expresses a past action with respect to the main clause verb.

> *Non credo che lui abbia capito.* / I don't believe he understood.
> *Non è possibile che loro siano già partiti.* / It's not possible that they have already left.
> *Benché sia venuta anche lei, non è felice.* / Although she too has come, he is not happy.

§8.5–3 Imperfect

> *L'imperfetto del congiuntivo*

The imperfect subjunctive is formed as follows.
   Drop the infinitive suffix and add the following endings.

Person	Endings		
	1st Conjugation = are	**2nd Conjugation** = ere	**3rd Conjugation** = ire
1st sing. (io)	-*assi*	-*essi*	-*issi*
2nd sing. (tu)	-*assi*	-*essi*	-*issi*
3rd sing. (lui/lei)	-*asse*	-*esse*	-*isse*
1st pl. (noi)	-*assimo*	-*essimo*	-*issimo*
2nd pl. (voi)	-*aste*	-*este*	-*iste*
3rd pl. (loro)	-*assero*	-*essero*	-*issero*

Conjugations

parlare / to speak → *parl-*

(io)	*parlassi* / I was speaking, I used to speak
(tu)	*parlassi* / you were speaking, you used to speak
(lui/lei)	*parlasse* / he, she, you (pol.) was/were speaking, he, she, you (pol.) used to speak
(noi)	*parlassimo* / we were speaking, we used to speak
(voi)	*parlaste* / you were speaking, you used to speak
(loro)	*parlassero* / they were speaking, they used to speak

scrivere / to write → *scriv-*

(io)	*scrivessi* / I was writing, I used to write
(tu)	*scrivessi* / you were writing, you used to write
(lui/lei)	*scrivesse* / he, she, you (pol.) was/were writing, he, she, you (pol.) used to write
(noi)	*scrivessimo* / we were writing, we used to write
(voi)	*scriveste* / you were writing, you used to write
(loro)	*scrivessero* / they were writing, they used to write

finire / to finish → *fin-*

(io)	*finissi* / I was finishing, I used to finish
(tu)	*finissi* / you were finishing, you used to finish
(lui/lei)	*finisse* / he, she, you (pol.) was/were finishing,
		he, she, you (pol.) used to finish
(noi)	*finissimo* / we were finishing, we used to finish
(voi)	*finiste* / you were finishing, you used to finish
(loro)	*finissero* / they were finishing, they used to finish

As in the use of the imperfect indicative (see §8.2–3), the imperfect subjunctive conveys the idea of repeated action in the past.

Tip

Essentially, if the main clause verb is in a past tense then the verb in the subordinate clause is generally in the imperfect subjunctive.

Present		**Past**
|		|
Spero	*che*	*abbia capito.* / I hope that he has understood.

Past		**Imperfect**
|		|
Speravo	*che*	*avesse capito.* / I was hoping that he (had) understood.

Examples

Mi sembrava che lui dicesse la verità. / It seemed to me that he was telling the truth.

Benché piovesse ieri, sono uscito lo stesso. / Although it was raining yesterday, I went out just the same.

The imperfect subjunctive is also used after *se* (if) in counter-factual statements when the main clause verb is in the conditional.

> *Se tu andassi a Roma, vedresti il Colosseo.* / If you were to go to Rome, you would see the Coliseum.
> *Se potessimo, andremmo in Italia subito.* / If we could, we would go to Italy right away.

It is also used in sentences beginning with *magari* (if only) expressing a wish or desire.

> *Magari non piovesse!* / If only it wouldn't rain!
> *Magari vincessi la lotteria!* / If only I would win the lottery!

§8.5–4 Pluperfect

> *Il trapassato del congiuntivo*

The *pluperfect subjunctive* corresponds to the pluperfect indicative (see §8.2–5). It is a formed with the imperfect subjunctive of the auxiliary verb plus the past participle of the verb, in that order.

> *avessi mangiato* / I had eaten
>
> *avessi* = auxiliary verb in the imperfect subjunctive
> *mangiato* = past participle
>
> *fossi andato* / I had gone
>
> *fossi* = auxiliary verb in the imperfect subjunctive
> *andato* = part participle

In the imperfect subjunctive, the auxiliary verbs are conjugated as follows:

	avere		*essere*	
io	avessi	I used to have	fossi	I used to be
tu	avessi	you used have	fossi	you used to be
lui/lei	avesse	he/she has, you used to have	fosse	he/she you used to be
noi	avessimo	we used to have	fossimo	we used to be
voi	aveste	you used to have	foste	you used to be
loro	avessero	they used to have	fossero	they used to be

Conjugations of verbs with *avere*

parlare / to speak → *parlato*

(io)	avessi parlato / I had spoken
(tu)	avessi parlato / you had spoken
(lui/lei)	avesse parlato / he, she, you (pol.) had spoken
(noi)	avessimo parlato / we had spoken
(voi)	aveste parlato / you had spoken
(loro)	avessero parlato / they had spoken

vendere / to sell → *venduto*

(io)	avessi venduto/ I had sold
(tu)	avessi venduto / you had sold
(lui/lei)	avesse venduto / he, she, you (pol.) had sold
(noi)	avessimo venduto / we had sold
(voi)	aveste venduto / you had sold
(loro)	avessero venduto / they had sold

dormire / to sleep → *dormito*

(io)	avessi dormito / I had slept
(tu)	avessi dormito / you had slept
(lui/lei)	avesse dormito / he, she, you (pol.) had slept

(noi)	*avessimo dormito* / we had slept
(voi)	*aveste dormito* / you had slept
(loro)	*avessero dormito* / they had slept

Conjugations of verbs with *essere*

arrivare / to arrive → *arrivato*

(io)	*fossi arrivato (-a)* / I had arrived
(tu)	*fossi arrivato (-a)* / you had arrived
(lui/lei)	*fosse arrivato (-a)* / he, she, you (pol.) had arrived
(noi)	*fossimo arrivati (-e)* / we had arrived
(voi)	*foste arrivati (-e)* / you had arrived
(loro)	*fossero arrivati (-e)* / they had arrived

cadere / to fall → *caduto*

(io)	*fossi caduto (-a)*/ I had fallen
(tu)	*fossi caduto (-a)*/ you had fallen
(lui/lei)	*fosse caduto (-a)* / he, she, you (pol.) had fallen
(noi)	*fossimo caduti (-e)* / we had fallen
(voi)	*foste caduti (-e)* / you had fallen
(loro)	*fossero caduti (-e)* / they had fallen

partire / to leave → *partito*

(io)	*fossi partito (-a)* / I had left
(tu)	*fossi partito (-a)* / you had left
(lui/lei)	*fosse partito (-a)* / he, she, you (pol.) had left
(noi)	*fossimo partiti (-e)* / we had left
(voi)	*foste partiti (-e)* / you had left
(loro)	*fossero partiti (-e)* / they had left

This tense corresponds to the pluperfect indicative (see §8.2–5) in usage. It allows you to express a past action that occurred before another past action.

Examples

Mi era sembrato che lui avesse detto la verità. / It seemed to me that he had said the truth.

Eravamo contenti che voi foste venuti. / We were happy that you had come.

Benché avesse piovuto tutto il mese, andavamo sempre fuori. / Although it had rained the entire month, we went out just the same.

As was the case with the imperfect subjunctive (see §8.5–3), the pluperfect subjunctive is also used after *se* (if) in counterfactual statements. In this case, it is used when the main clause verb is in the conditional.

> *Se avessi avuto i soldi, l'avrei comprata.* / If I had had the money, I would have bought it.
>
> *Se tu avessi studiato ieri, oggi non ti preoccuperesti.* / If you had studied yesterday, today you wouldn't worry.

§8.6 THE INDEFINITE TENSES

> *I tempi indefiniti*

The *indefinite* tenses allow you to express actions that refer to indefinite time relations—"to do something"; "doing something"; etc.

§8.6–1 The Infinitive

> *L'infinito*

Recall from §8.1 that there are three main types of infinitives in Italian:

First Conjugation	Second Conjugation	Third Conjugation
parlare / to speak	*scrivere* / to write	*capire* / to understand
arrivare / to arrive	*prendere* / to take	*aprire* / to open

There is a fourth type ending in *-rre*; but there are very few of them:

produrre / to produce
tradurre / to translate
porre / to put
trarre / to pull

All verbs of this type have irregular conjugations.

Person	produrre	porre	trarre
1st sing. (io)	produco	pongo	traggo
2nd sing. (tu)	produci	poni	trai
3rd sing. (lui/lei)	produce	pone	trae
1st pl. (noi)	produciamo	poniamo	traiamo
2nd pl. (voi)	producete	ponete	traete
3rd pl. (loro)	producono	pongono	traggono

There is also a *past infinitive* consisting of an auxiliary verb in the infinitive and a past participle.

> *aver(e) parlato* / having spoken *esser(e) arrivato (-a)* / having arrived
>
> *aver(e) venduto* / having sold *esser(e) caduto (-a)* / having fallen
>
> *aver(e) dormito* / having slept *esser(e) partito (-a)* / having left

Note that the final -*e* of the auxiliary may be dropped.

Examples

> *Dopo aver mangiato, uscirò.* / After having eaten, I will go out.
>
> *Dopo esser arrivati, sono andati al cinema.* / After having arrived, they went to the movies.

Recall that object pronouns are (usually) attached to infinitives (review §7.3–2):

> *Invece di mangiarlo, l'ho dato a lei.* / Instead of eating it, I gave it to her.

The infinitive can function as a substantive, in which case it is always assigned a masculine gender.

> *Il mangiare è necessario per vivere.* / Eating is necessary to live.

When the subjects of two clauses are the same, then the infinitive is used.

Different Subjects	The Same Subjects
Lui crede che io scriva bene. / He believes that I write well.	*Lui crede di scrivere bene.* / He believes that he (himself) writes well.

§8.6–2 The Gerund

Il gerundio

The *gerund* is formed by dropping the infinitive endings and adding the following endings to the stem:

parlare / to speak → *parl-* → *parlando* / speaking
scrivere / to write → *scrive-* → *scrivendo* / writing
finire / to finish → *fin-* → *finendo* / finishing

The most important use of the gerund is in progressive tenses, which are made up of the verb *stare* plus the gerund.

Person	Present Progressive (Indicative)		
	1st Conjugation	**2nd Conjugation**	**3rd Conjugation**
1st sing. (io)	*sto mangiando* / I am eating	*sto scrivendo* / I am writing	*sto finendo* / I am finishing
2nd sing. (tu)	*stai mangiando* / you are eating	*stai scrivendo* / you are writing	*stai finendo* / you are finishing
3rd sing. (lui/lei)	*sta mangiando* / he, she, you (pol.) is/are eating	*sta scrivendo* / he, she, you (pol.) is/are writing	*sta finendo* / he, she, you (pol.) is/are finishing
1st pl. (noi)	*stiamo mangiando* / we are eating	*stiamo scrivendo* / we are writing	*stiamo finendo* / we are finishing
2nd pl. (voi)	*state mangiando* / you are eating	*state scrivendo* / you are writing	*state finendo* / you are finishing
3rd pl. (loro)	*stanno mangiando* / they are eating	*stanno scrivendo* / they are writing	*stanno finendo* / they are finishing

This tense is an alternative to the present indicative, allowing you to zero in on an ongoing action.

> *In questo momento, mia sorella sta mangiando.* / At this moment, my sister is eating.

Person	Imperfect Progressive (Indicative)		
	1st Conjugation	**2nd Conjugation**	**3rd Conjugation**
1st sing. (io)	*stavo mangiando* / I was eating	*stavo scrivendo* / I was writing	*stavo finendo* / I was finishing
2nd sing. (tu)	*stavi mangiando* / you were eating	*stavi scrivendo* / you were writing	*stavi finendo* / you were finishing
3rd sing. (lui/lei)	*stava mangiando* / he, she, you (pol.) is/were eating	*stava scrivendo* / he, she, you (pol.) is/were writing	*stava finendo* / he, she, you (pol.) is/were finishing
1st pl. (noi)	*stavamo mangiando* / we were eating	*stavamo scrivendo* / we were writing	*stavamo finendo* / we were finishing
2nd pl. (voi)	*stavate mangiando* / you were eating	*stavate scrivendo* / you were writing	*stavate finendo* / you were finishing
3rd pl. (loro)	*stavano mangiando* / they were eating	*stavano scrivendo* / they were writing	*stavano finendo* / they were finishing

Examples

> *Ieri mia sorella stava mangiando, quando è arrivata la zia.* / My sister was eating yesterday, when our aunt arrived.
> *Cosa stavi facendo ieri, quando ti ho telefonato?* / What were you doing yesterday, when I phoned you?

Person	Present Progressive Subjunctive		
	1st Conjugation	2nd Conjugation	3rd Conjugation
1st sing. (io)	*stia mangiando* / I am eating	*stia scrivendo* / I am writing	*stia finendo* / I am finishing
2nd sing. (tu)	*stai mangiando* / you are eating	*stai scrivendo* / you are writing	*stai finendo* / you are finishing
3rd sing. (lui/lei)	*stia mangiando* / he, she, you (pol.) is/are eating	*stia scrivendo* / he, she, you (pol.) is/are writing	*stia finendo* / he, she, you (pol.) is/are finishing
1st pl. (noi)	*stiamo mangiando* / we are eating	*stiamo scrivendo* / we are writing	*stiamo finendo* / we are finishing
2nd pl. (voi)	*stiate mangiando* / you are eating	*stiate scrivendo* / you are writing	*stiate finendo* / you are finishing
3rd pl. (loro)	*stiano mangiando* / they are eating	*stiano scrivendo* / they are writing	*stiano finendo* / they are finishing

This tense is an alternative to the present subjunctive, allowing you to zero in on an ongoing action.

> *Penso che in questo momento, mia sorella stia mangiando.* / I think that at this moment, my sister is eating.

Person	Imperfect Progressive Subjunctive		
	1st Conjugation	**2nd Conjugation**	**3rd Conjugation**
1st sing. (io)	*stessi mangiando* / I was eating	*stessi scrivendo* / I was writing	*stessi finendo* / I was finishing
2nd sing. (tu)	*stessi mangiando* / you were eating	*stessi scrivendo* / you were writing	*stessi finendo* / you were finishing
3rd sing. (lui/lei)	*stesse mangiando* / he, she, you (pol.) is/were eating	*stesse scrivendo* / he, she, you (pol.) is/were writing	*stesse finendo* / he, she, you (pol.) is/were finishing
1st pl. (noi)	*stessimo mangiando* / we were eating	*stessimo scrivendo* / we were writing	*stessimo finendo* / we were finishing
2nd pl. (voi)	*steste mangiando* / you were eating	*steste scrivendo* / you were writing	*steste finendo* / you were finishing
3rd pl. (loro)	*stessero mangiando* / they were eating	*stessero scrivendo* / they were writing	*stessero finendo* / they were finishing

Examples

> *Penso che ieri mia sorella stesse mangiando, quando è arrivata la zia.* / I think my sister was eating yesterday, when our aunt arrived.
>
> *Non so cosa stesse facendo ieri, quando le ho telefonato.* / I do not know what she was doing yesterday, when I phoned her.

The gerund is also used, as in English, to express indefinite actions, replacing *mentre* (while) + imperfect when the subject of the two clauses is the same.

> *Mentre camminavo, ho visto Marco.* / While I was walking, I saw Mark.

or

> *Camminando, ho visto Marco.* / While walking, I saw Mark.

Recall that object pronouns are attached to the gerund (see §7.3–2).

> *Vedendolo, l'ho salutato.* / Upon seeing him, I greeted him.

There is also a *past gerund*, consisting of an auxiliary verb in the gerund and a past participle.

avendo parlato / having spoken	*essendo arrivato (-a)* / having arrived
avendo venduto / having sold	*essendo caduto (-a)* / having fallen
avendo dormito / having slept	*essendo partito (-a)* / having left

Examples

> *Avendo mangiato tutto, siamo usciti.* / Having eaten everything, we went out.
> *Essendo andati in Italia, visitarono tanti bei posti.* / Having gone to Italy, they visited many nice places.

§8.7 REFLEXIVE VERBS

> *I verbi riflessivi*

A *reflexive* verb is a verb, in any tense or mood, that requires reflexive pronouns (review §7.2–3). More technically, it is a verb having an identical subject and direct object, as in "She dressed herself."

A reflexive infinitive is identifiable by the ending *-si* (oneself).

lavarsi / to wash oneself *divertirsi* / to enjoy oneself

Reflexive verbs are conjugated in exactly the same manner as reflexive verbs with, of course, reflexive pronouns (review §7.2–3).

Examples

Mi alzo presto ogni giorno. / I get up early every day.

Ci divertivamo sempre da bambini. / We always used to have fun as children.

Sembra che tu ti diverta sempre in Italia. / It seems that you always enjoy yourself in Italy.

Person	Present Indicative		
	alzarsi / to get up	*mettersi* / to put on	*divertirsi* / to enjoy oneself
1st sing. (io)	*mi alzo*	*mi metto*	*mi diverto*
2nd sing. (tu)	*ti alzi*	*ti metti*	*ti diverti*
3rd sing. (lui/lei)	*si alza*	*si mette*	*si diverte*
1st pl. (noi)	*ci alziamo*	*ci mettiamo*	*ci divertiamo*
2nd pl. (voi)	*vi alzate*	*vi mettete*	*vi divertite*
3rd pl. (loro)	*si alzano*	*si mettono*	*si divertono*

For the relevant uses and functions of the present indicative review §8.2–1

Person	Imperfect Indicative		
	alzarsi / to get up	*mettersi* / to put on	*divertirsi* / to enjoy oneself
1st sing. (io)	*mi alzavo*	*mi mettevo*	*mi divertivo*
2nd sing. (tu)	*ti alzavi*	*ti mettevi*	*ti divertivi*
3rd sing. (lui/lei)	*si alzava*	*si metteva*	*si divertiva*
1st pl. (noi)	*ci alzavamo*	*ci mettevamo*	*ci divertivamo*
2nd pl. (voi)	*vi alzavate*	*vi mettevate*	*vi divertivate*
3rd pl. (loro)	*si alzavano*	*si mettevano*	*si divertivano*

For the relevant uses and functions of the imperfect indicative review §8.2–3

Person	Past Absolute		
	alzarsi / to get up	*doversi* / to have to do something oneself	*divertirsi* / to enjoy oneself
1st sing. (io)	*mi alzai*	*mi dovei (dovetti)*	*mi divertii*
2nd sing. (tu)	*ti alzasti*	*ti dovesti*	*ti divertisti*
3rd sing. (lui/lei)	*si alzò*	*si dovè (dovette)*	*si divertì*
1st pl. (noi)	*ci alzammo*	*ci dovemmo*	*divertimmo*
2nd pl. (voi)	*vi alzaste*	*vi doveste*	*divertiste*
3rd pl. (loro)	*si alzarono*	*si doverono (dovettero)*	*si divertirono*

For the relevant uses and functions of the past absolute review §8.2–4

Person	Simple Future		
	alzarsi / **to get up**	*mettersi /* **to put on**	*divertirsi /* **to enjoy oneself**
1st sing. (io)	*mi alzerò*	*mi metterò*	*mi divertirò*
2nd sing. (tu)	*ti alzerai*	*ti metterai*	*ti divertirai*
3rd sing. (lui/lei)	*si alzerà*	*si metterà*	*si divertirà*
1st pl. (noi)	*ci alzeremo*	*ci metteremo*	*ci divertiremo*
2nd pl. (voi)	*vi alzerete*	*vi metterete*	*vi divertirete*
3rd pl. (loro)	*si alzeranno*	*si metteranno*	*si divertiranno*

For the relevant uses and functions of the simple future review §8.2–6

Person	Imperative		
	alzarsi / to get up	*mettersi /* to put on	*divertirsi /* to enjoy oneself
1st sing. (io)	—	—	—
2nd sing. (tu)	*alzati non alzarti/non ti alzare*	*mettiti non metterti/non ti mettere*	*divertiti non divertirti/non ti divertire*
3rd sing. (lui/lei)	*si alzi*	*si metta*	*si diverta*
1st pl. (noi)	*alziamoci*	*mettiamoci*	*divertiamoci*
2nd pl. (voi)	*alzatevi*	*mettetevi*	*divertitevi*
3rd pl. (loro)	*si alzino*	*si mettano*	*si divertano*

For the relevant uses and functions of the imperative review §8.3

Person	Conditional		
	alzarsi / to get up	*mettersi* / to put on	*divertirsi* / to enjoy oneself
1st sing. (io)	*mi alzerei*	*mi metterei*	*mi divertirei*
2nd sing. (tu)	*ti alzeresti*	*ti metteresti*	*ti divertiresti*
3rd sing. (lui/lei)	*si alzerebbe*	*si metterebbe*	*si divertirebbe*
1st pl. (noi)	*ci alzeremmo*	*ci metteremmo*	*ci divertiremmo*
2nd pl. (voi)	*vi alzereste*	*vi mettereste*	*vi divertireste*
3rd pl. (loro)	*si alzerebbero*	*si metterebbero*	*si divertirebbero*

For the relevant uses and functions of the conditional review
§8.4–1

Person	Present Subjunctive		
	alzarsi / to get up	*mettersi* / to put on	*divertirsi* / to enjoy oneself
1st sing. (io)	*mi alzi*	*mi metta*	*mi diverta*
2nd sing. (tu)	*ti alzi*	*ti metta*	*ti diverta*
3rd sing. (lui/lei)	*si alzi*	*si metta*	*si diverta*
1st pl. (noi)	*ci alziamo*	*ci mettiamo*	*ci divertiamo*
2nd pl. (voi)	*vi alziate*	*vi mettiate*	*vi divertiate*
3rd pl. (loro)	*si alzino*	*si mettano*	*si divertano*

For the relevant uses and functions of the present subjunctive review §8.5–1

Person	Imperfect Subjunctive		
	alzarsi / to get up	*mettersi* / to put on	*divertirsi* / to enjoy oneself
1st sing. (io)	mi alzassi	mi mettessi	mi divertissi
2nd sing. (tu)	ti alzassi	ti mettessi	ti divertissi
3rd sing. (lui/lei)	si alzasse	si mettesse	si divertisse
1st pl. (noi)	ci alzasssimo	ci mettessimo	ci divertissimo
2nd pl. (voi)	vi alzaste	vi metteste	vi divertiste
3rd pl. (loro)	si alzassero	si mettessero	si divertissero

For the relevant uses and functions of the imperfect subjunctive review §8.5–3

In compound tenses, all reflexive verbs are conjugated with *essere*.

Present Perfect
alzarsi
(io)   mi sono alzato (-a)
(tu)   ti sei alzato (-a)
(lui/lei) si è alzato (-a)
(noi)   ci siamo alzati (-e)
(voi)   vi siete alzati (-e)
(loro)   si sono alzati (-e)

mettersi (irregular past participle = *messo*)
(io)   mi sono messo (-a)
(tu)   ti sei messo (-a)
(lui/lei) si è messo (-a)

(noi)	*ci siamo messi (-e)*
(voi)	*vi siete messi (-e)*
(loro)	*si sono messi (-e)*

divertirsi

(io)	*mi sono divertito (-a)*
(tu)	*ti sei divertito (-a)*
(lui/lei)	*si è divertito (-a)*
(noi)	*ci siamo divertiti (-e)*
(voi)	*vi siete divertiti (-e)*
(loro)	*si sono divertiti (-e)*

For the relevant uses and functions of the present perfect review §8.2–2

Pluperfect Indicative
alzarsi

(io)	*mi ero alzato (-a)*
(tu)	*ti eri alzato (-a)*
(lui/lei)	*si era alzato (-a)*
(noi)	*ci eravamo alzati (-e)*
(voi)	*vi eravate alzati (-e)*
(loro)	*si erano alzati (-e)*

mettersi (irregular past participle = *messo*)

(io)	*mi ero messo (-a)*
(tu)	*ti eri messo (-a)*
(lui/lei)	*si era messo (-a)*
(noi)	*ci eravamo messi (-e)*
(voi)	*vi eravate messi (-e)*
(loro)	*si erano messi (-e)*

divertirsi

(io)	*mi ero divertito (-a)*
(tu)	*ti eri divertito (-a)*
(lui/lei)	*si era divertito (-a)*
(noi)	*ci eravamo divertiti (-e)*
(voi)	*vi eravate divertiti (-e)*
(loro)	*si erano divertiti (-e)*

For the relevant uses and functions of the pluperfect indicative review §8.2–5

Future Perfect

alzarsi

(io)	*mi sarò alzato (-a)*
(tu)	*ti sarai alzato (-a)*
(lui/lei)	*si sarà alzato (-a)*
(noi)	*ci saremo alzati (-e)*
(voi)	*vi sarete alzati (-e)*
(loro)	*si saranno alzati (-e)*

mettersi (irregular past participle = *messo*)

(io)	*mi sarò messo (-a)*
(tu)	*ti sarai messo (-a)*
(lui/lei)	*si sarà messo (-a)*
(noi)	*ci saremo messi (-e)*
(voi)	*vi sarete messi (-e)*
(loro)	*si saranno messi (-e)*

divertirsi

(io)	*mi sarò divertito (-a)*
(tu)	*ti sarai divertito (-a)*
(lui/lei)	*si sarà divertito (-a)*
(noi)	*ci saremo divertiti (-e)*
(voi)	*vi sarete divertiti (-e)*
(loro)	*si saranno divertiti (-e)*

For the relevant uses and functions of the future perfect review §8.2–7

Conditional Perfect

alzarsi

(io)	*mi sarei alzato (-a)*
(tu)	*ti saresti alzato (-a)*
(lui/lei)	*si sarebbe alzato (-a)*
(noi)	*ci saremmo alzati (-e)*
(voi)	*vi sareste alzati (-e)*
(loro)	*si sarebbero alzati (-e)*

mettersi (irregular past participle = *messo*)

(io)	*mi sarei messo (-a)*
(tu)	*ti saresti messo (-a)*
(lui/lei)	*si sarebbe messo (-a)*

(noi)	ci saremmo messi (-e)
(voi)	vi sareste messi (-e)
(loro)	si sarebbero messi (-e)

divertirsi

(io)	mi sarei divertito (-a)
(tu)	ti saresti divertito (-a)
(lui/lei)	si sarebbe divertito (-a)
(noi)	ci saremmo divertiti (-e)
(voi)	vi sareste divertiti (-e)
(loro)	si sarebbero divertiti (-e)

For the relevant uses and functions of the conditional review
§8.4–2

Past Subjunctive

alzarsi

(io)	mi sia alzato (-a)
(tu)	ti sia alzato (-a)
(lui/lei)	si sia alzato (-a)
(noi)	ci siamo alzati (-e)
(voi)	vi siate alzati (-e)
(loro)	si siano alzati (-e)

mettersi (irregular past participle = *messo*)

(io)	mi sia messo (-a)
(tu)	ti sia messo (-a)
(lui/lei)	si sia messo (-a)
(noi)	ci siamo messi (-e)
(voi)	vi siate messi (-e)
(loro)	si siano messi (-e)

divertirsi

(io)	mi sia divertito (-a)
(tu)	ti sia divertito (-a)
(lui/lei)	si sia divertito (-a)
(noi)	ci siamo divertiti (-e)
(voi)	vi siate divertiti (-e)
(loro)	si siano divertiti (-e)

For the relevant uses and functions of the past subjunctive
review §8.5–2

Pluperfect Subjunctive

alzarsi

(io)	*mi fossi alzato (-a)*
(tu)	*ti fossi alzato (-a)*
(lui/lei)	*si fosse alzato (-a)*
(noi)	*ci fossimo alzati (-e)*
(voi)	*vi foste alzati (-e)*
(loro)	*si fossero alzati (-e)*

mettersi (irregular past participle = *messo*)

(io)	*mi fossi messo (-a)*
(tu)	*ti fossi messo (-a)*
(lui/lei)	*si fosse messo (-a)*
(noi)	*ci fossimo messi (-e)*
(voi)	*vi foste messi (-e)*
(loro)	*si fossero messi (-e)*

divertirsi

(io)	*mi fossi divertito (-a)*
(tu)	*ti fossi divertito (-a)*
(lui/lei)	*si fosse divertito (-a)*
(noi)	*ci fossimo divertiti (-e)*
(voi)	*vi foste divertiti (-e)*
(loro)	*si fossero divertiti (-e)*

For the relevant uses and functions of the pluperfect subjunctive review §8.5–4

Common Reflexive Verbs

alzarsi / to get up, wake up, stand up
annoiarsi / to become bored
arrabbiarsi / to become angry
dimenticarsi / to forget
divertirsi / to enjoy oneself, have fun
lamentarsi / to complain
lavarsi / to wash oneself
mettersi / to put on, wear, set about, begin to
prepararsi / to prepare oneself
sentirsi / to feel
sposarsi / to marry, get married
svegliarsi / to wake up
vergognarsi / to be ashamed

§8.8 THE PASSIVE VOICE

Il passivo

Any active verb can be turned into a corresponding passive form (§2.2–5).

1. Change the order of the subject and the object:

Alessandro mangia la mela. / Alexander is eating the apple.

La mela (mangia) Alessandro

2. Change the verb into the passive form by introducing the auxiliary verb *essere* in the same tense and mood and changing the verb into its past participle form. Recall that verbs conjugated with *essere* agree with the subject (§8.2–2).

La mela è mangiata (Alessandro).

3. Put *da* (by) in front of the passive object.

La mela è mangiata da Alessandro. / The apple is eaten by Alexander.

Examples

Active	**Passive**
La ragazza ha letto quel libro. / The girl read that book.	*Quel libro è letto dalla ragazza.* / That book is read by the girl.
Quell'uomo comprerà la FIAT. / That man will buy the FIAT.	*La FIAT sarà comprata da quell'uomo.* / The FIAT will be bought by that man.
Io scrissi quella lettera. / I wrote that letter.	*Quella lettera fu scritta da me.* / That letter was written by me.

§8.9 MODAL VERBS

The verbs *potere* (to be able to), *dovere* (to have to), and *volere* (to want to) are *modal* verbs—that is, they are verbs that inject a mode (willingness, necessity, etc.) of doing, saying, acting, etc. to the predicate.

Examples

Posso venire anch'io? / Can I come too?
Ma non dovevi andare in Italia? / Didn't you have to go to Italy?
Vorrei comprare un nuovo computer. / I would like to buy a new computer.

Modal verbs are irregular. You can look up their forms in the *Verb Charts* section at the back of this book.

Keep the following in mind.

In compound tenses, the auxiliary verb is determined by the infinitive that follows a modal.

Verb Conjugated with *avere*	**Verb Conjugated with *essere***
Non ha voluto vedere Firenze. / He didn't want to see Florence.	*Non è voluto andare a Firenze.* / He didn't want to go to Florence.

However, in conversational Italian, the tendency is to use only *avere*.

Non è voluto uscire. / He didn't want to go out.

or
Non ha voluto uscire. / He didn't want to go out.

Object pronouns can be put before the modals or attached on to the infinitive (§7.3–2):

La voglio mangiare. / I want to eat it.

or
Voglio mangiarla. / I want to eat it.

This applies to reflexive pronouns as well. In compound tenses, the choice of *avere* or *essere* is dictated by whether the reflexive pronoun does or does not precede the past participle of the verb. If it precedes, *essere* is used; if it does not, then *avere* is used.

Before	**After**
Maria non si è potuta divertire. / Mary was unable to enjoy herself.	*Maria non ha potuto divertirsi.* / Mary was unable to enjoy herself.

In the present conditional, these verbs translate as "could," "would," and "should," and in the past conditional as "could have," "would have," and "should have":

Lo potrei fare. / I could do it.
Lo avrei potuto fare. / I could have done it.
Lo vorrei fare. / I would do it.
Lo avrei voluto fare. / I would have done it.
Lo dovrei fare. / I should do it.
Lo avrei dovuto fare. / I should have done it.

§9.

Adverbs

§9.1 WHAT ARE ADVERBS?

Gli avverbi

Adverbs are words that modify verbs, adjectives, or other adverbs. They convey relations of time, place, degree of intensity, and manner.

Mara guida lentamente. / Mara drives slowly.
   ↑   ↑
  verb   adverb

Questa casa è molto bella. / This house is very beautiful.
              ↑   ↑
          adverb   adjective

Giovanni guida troppo lentamente. / John drives too slowly.
                 ↑   ↑
              adverb   adverb

§9.2 ADVERBS OF MANNER

Adverbs of manner are formed in the following way. Notice that the ending *-mente* corresponds to the English ending "-ly."

Change the *-o* ending of a descriptive adjective (see §6.2) to *-a*:
certo / certain   →   *certa*
lento / slow   →   *lenta*

Add *-mente*:
certa   →   *certamente* /certainly
lenta   →   *lentamente* /slowly

If the adjective ends in -*e*, instead of -*o*, then simply add on -*mente*:

elegante / elegant	→	*elegantemente* / elegantly
semplice / simple	→	*semplicemente* /simply

However, if the adjective ends in -*le* or -*re* and is preceded by a vowel, then the -*e* is dropped:

facile / easy	→	*facilmente* /easily
popolare / popular	→	*popolarmente* / popularly

A few exceptions to these rules are:

benevolo / benevolent	→	*benevolmente* / benevolently
leggero / light	→	*leggermente* / lightly
violento / violent	→	*violentemente* / violently

Examples

Adjective	**Adverb of Manner**
enorme / enormous	*tristemente* / sadly
felice / happy	*felicemente* / happily
preciso / precise	*precisamente* / precisely
raro / rare	*raramente* /rarely
regolare / regular	*regolarmente* / regularly
speciale / special	*specialmente* / specially
triste / sad	*tristemente* / sadly
utile / useful	*utilmente* / usefully
vero / true	*veramente* / truly

These adjectives normally follow the verb, but may begin a sentence for emphasis.

> *Lui manda e-mail ai suoi amici regolarmente.* / He sends his friends e-mails regularly.
>
> *Regolarmente, lui manda e-mail ai suoi amici.* / Regularly, he sends his friends e-mails.

§9.3 OTHER KINDS OF ADVERBS

Adverbs of all kinds are needed for various conversational purposes. Some very useful ones are provided in the following chart.

abbastanza / enough	*nel frattempo* / in the meanwhile
allora / then	*oggi* / today
anche / also, too	*oggigiorno* / nowadays
ancora / still, yet, again	*ormai* / by now
anzi / as a matter of fact	*per caso* / by chance
appena / just, barely	*piuttosto* / rather
di nuovo / again	*poi* / then, after
domani / tomorrow	*presto* / early
finora / until now	*prima* / first
fra (tra) poco / in a little while	*purtroppo* / unfortunately
già / already	*quasi* / almost
in fretta / in a hurry	*solo* / only
insieme / together	*stamani* / this morning
invece / instead	*stasera* / this evening
lì, là / there	*subito* / right away
lontano / far	*tardi* / late
male / bad(ly)	*vicino* / near(by)

Examples

Noi andiamo spesso al cinema. / We often go to the movies.
L'ha fatto ancora una volta. / He did it again (one more time).
Lei abita lontano, e lui vicino. / She lives far, and he nearby.
Sono quasi le tre. / It's almost three o'clock.
Ho appena finito di lavorare. / I have just finished working.
Prima mangio e poi studio. / First I will eat, and then I will study.

In compound tenses (see §8.2-2), some of these adverbs can be put between the auxiliary verb and the past participle. The ones most commonly placed in this way are *ancora*, *appena*, and *già*.

Examples

Sono già usciti. / They went out already.
Ha appena telefonato. / She has just phoned.
Non abbiamo ancora finito di lavorare. / We haven't yet finished working.

The adjectives *molto, tanto, poco, troppo,* and *parecchio* (see §6.4-4) can also be used as adverbs. But be careful! In this case, there is no agreement to be made!

Adjectives	**Adverbs**
Lei ha molti soldi. / She has a lot of money.	*Lei è molto intelligente.* / She is very intelligent.
Lei ha molta fame. / She is very hungry.	*Lei è molto famosa.* / She is very famous.
Ci sono pochi studenti qui. / There are few students here.	*Loro studiano poco.* / They study little.

Tip

To determine if a word such as *molto* is an adjective or adverb, check the following word. If it is a noun, then *molto* is an adjective, agreeing with the noun. Otherwise it can be either an adverb or pronoun. In either case, no agreement pattern is required.

Lei ha molti soldi. / She has a lot of money.
       noun

---

§9.4 THE COMPARISON OF ADVERBS

Adverbs are compared in the same manner as adjectives. So, review §6.5.

Examples

lentamente / slowly	*più lentamente* / more slowly
facilmente / easily	*meno facilmente* / less easily
lontano / far	*il più lontano* / the farthest

Tricky Comparative Forms

Adjectives

buono / good	→	*più buono = migliore* / better
	→	*il migliore* / the best
cattivo / bad	→	*più cattivo = peggiore* / worse
	→	*il peggiore* / the worst

Adverbs

bene / well	→	*più bene = meglio* / better
	→	*il meglio* / the best
male / bad(ly)	→	*più male = peggio* / worse
	→	*il peggio* / the worst

Given that both the adjectives *buono* and *cattivo* and their corresponding adverb forms *bene* and *male* (above) are rendered in English by "better" and "worse," you might become confused about which form to use. Follow the tip.

Tip

migliore or *meglio*?

To figure out which form is the appropriate one, "go back" in your mind to the "uncompared" form in English

That wine is *better*. (compared form)

That wine is *good*. (uncompared form)

Now you can see that "better" in this case renders the comparative of the adjective *buono*.

Quel vino è migliore.

That watch works *better*. (compared form)

That watch works *well*. (uncompared form)

Now you can see that "better" in this case renders the comparative of the adverb *bene*.

Quell'orologio funziona meglio.

Use the exact same kind of "backward thinking" for *peggiore* versus *peggio*.

§10.
Prepositions

§10.1 WHAT ARE PREPOSITIONS?

> *Le preposizioni*

A *preposition* (literally, "a putting before") is a word that comes before some other part of speech, generally a noun, substantive, or noun phrase, to show its relationship to some other part in the sentence.

> *La bicicletta di Maria è nuova.* / Mary's bicycle is new.

> *Lui era in macchina.* / He was in the car.

§10.2 PREPOSITIONAL CONTRACTIONS

> *Le preposizioni articolate*

When the prepositions *a* (to, at), *di* (of), *da* (from), *in* (in), and *su* (on) immediately precede a definite article form (review §4.2-1), they contract with it to form one word.

> *Questo è il libro del cugino di Francesca.* / That is the book of Francesca's cousin.
> *del cugino = di + il (cugino)*
> *Ci sono due dollari nella scatola.* / There are two dollars in the box.
> *nella = in + la (scatola)*
> *Arrivano dall'Italia domani.* / They are arriving from Italy tomorrow.
> *dall' = da + l' (Italia)*

The following chart summarizes the different contracted forms.

+	il	i	lo	l'	gli	la	le
a	al	ai	allo	all'	agli	alla	alle
da	dal	dai	dallo	dall'	dagli	dalla	dalle
di	del	dei	dello	dell'	degli	della	delle
in	nel	nei	nello	nell'	negli	nella	nelle
su	sul	sui	sullo	sull'	sugli	sulla	sulle

Examples

I gioielli sono nel cassetto. / The jewels are in the drawer.
Ecco gli indirizzi elettronici degli amici miei. / Here are the electronic addresses of my friends.
Le forchette sono sulla tavola. / The forks are on the table.
Domani mio cugino andrà dal medico. / Tomorrow my cousin is going to the doctor's.
Arrivano alle nove di sera. / They are arriving at 9 p.m.

Contraction with the preposition *con* (with) is optional. In actual fact, only the forms *col* = *con* + *il* and *coll'* = *con* + *la* are found in current day Italian with any degree of frequency.

Examples

Lui parlerà col direttore domani. / He will speak with the director tomorrow.
Loro ariveranno coll'Alitalia. / They will arrive with Alitalia.

Other prepositions do not contract.

tra, fra / between, among
per / for, through
sopra / above, on top
sotto / under, below

Examples

Lo faccio per il principio. / I am doing it on principle.
L'ho messo tra la tavola e la sedia. / I put it between the table and the chair.

The article is dropped in expressions that have a high degree of usage or have become idiomatic.

> *Sono a casa.* / I am at home.
> *Vado in macchina.* / I'm going by car.

However, if the noun in such expressions is modified in any way whatsoever, then the article *must* be used.

> *Sono alla casa nuova di Michele.* / I am at Michael's new home.
> *Vado nella macchina di Luigi.* / I'm going in Louis' car.

§10.3 SOME USES

Prepositions have many, many uses. All of them cannot be mentioned here. The more important ones are listed below.

A

A is used in front of a city name to render the idea of "in a city."

> *Abito a Roma.* / I live in Rome.

Otherwise, *in* is used.

> *Vivo in Italia.* / I live in Italy.

Di

Di is used to indicate possession or relationship.

> *È la macchina nuova di Alessandro.* / It's Alex's new car.
> *Come si chiama la figlia del professore?* /
>   What's the name of the professor's daughter?

Da

Da corresponds to "from" and "to" in expressions such as the following.

> *Vado dal medico.* / I'm going to the doctor's.
> *Vengo dalla farmacia.* / I'm coming from the pharmacy.

It translates as both "since" and "from" in progressive temporal constructions.

> *Vivo qui dal 1998.* / I have been living here since 1998.
> *Vivo qui da undici anni.* / I have been living here for 11 years.

It also translates the English expression "as a . . ."

> *Te lo dico da amico.* / I'm telling you as a friend.
> *Da piccolo, navigavo spesso l'Internet.* / As a kid, I used to navigate the Internet often.

In expressions consisting of a noun + infinitive it is translated in various ways.

> *una macchina da vendere* / a car to sell
> *un abito da sera* / an evening dress

Per

Per is used in time expressions when "future duration" is implied.

> *Abiterò in questa città per tre anni.* / I will live in this city for three years.

A versus *di*

Some verbs are followed by *a* before an infinitive.

> *Cominciano a capire.* / They are starting to understand.
> *Devo imparare ad usare il computer.* / I must learn how to use the computer.

Some are followed instead by *di*.

> *Finiranno di lavorare alle sei.* / They will finish working at six o'clock.
> *Cercheremo di rientrare presto.* / We will try to get back early.

Others are not followed by a preposition.

> *Voglio capire meglio.* / I want to understand better.
> *Desiderano andare in Italia.* / They want to go to Italy.
> *Preferisco rimanere a casa stasera.* / I prefer staying home tonight.

 Tip

The only sure way to learn which preposition (if any) is used in a certain construction or idiomatic expression is to consult a good dictionary!

§11.
Negatives and Other Grammatical Points

§11.1 WHAT ARE NEGATIVES?

> *Forme negative*

Negatives are words that allow you to deny, refuse, or oppose something.

> *Non conosco nessuno qui.* / I do not know anyone here.
> *Non lo faccio più.* / I won't do it anymore.

§11.2 COMMON NEGATIVES

Recall that any sentence can be made negative in Italian by simply putting *non* before the predicate (see §2.1-2). The following are some common negative constructions. Notice that *non* is retained before the predicate.

non . . . mai / never	
non . . . nessuno / no one	
non . . . niente, nulla / nothing	
non . . . più / no more, no longer	
non . . . neanche, nemmeno, neppure / not even	
non . . . né . . . né / neither . . . nor	
non . . . mica / not really, quite	

Examples

Affirmative	**Negative**
Lui canta sempre. / He always sings.	*Lui non canta mai.* / He never sings.
Qualcuno sta chiamando. / Someone is calling.	*Non sta chiamando nessuno.* / No one is calling.

Ci vado spesso. / I go there   *Non ci vado mai.* / I never go
    a lot.   there.

A negative can be put at the beginning of a sentence for
emphasis. In this case, the *non* is dropped.

Nessuno parla! / No one is speaking.
Mai capirò i verbi! / Never will I understand verbs!

§11.3   OTHER GRAMMATICAL POINTS

The conjunctions *e* (and) and *o* (or) allow you to join up similar
parts of speech (two nouns, two phrases, etc.)

Marco e Carlo sono amici o nemici. / Mark and Charles are
    friends or enemies.

The conjunction *e* and the preposition *a* can be changed to *ed*
and *ad*, respectively, before a word beginning with a vowel.
This makes the pronunciation smoother.

Gina ed Elena sono buone amiche. / Gina and Helen are good
    friends.
Noi vivamo ad Atene. / We live in Athens.

Be careful with the following confusingly similar structures!

Singular	Plural
Che cosa è? / What is it?	*Che cosa sono?* / What are they?
È un libro. / It's a book.	*Sono dei libri.* / They are books.
C'è Alessandro? / Is Alex there?	*Ci sono Alessandro e Sara?* / Are Alex and Sarah there?
Sì, c'è. / Yes, he is (here).	*Sì, ci sono.* / Yes, they are (here).
Dov'è Alessandro? / Where is Alex?	*Dove sono Alessandro e Sara?* / Where are Alex and Sara?
Ecco Alessandro. / Here's Alex.	*Eccoli.* / Here they are.

The verb *fare* (to do, make) can be used in *causative* constructions. The most common of these is the following.

Maria fa lavare i piatti a suo fratello. / Mary has her brother wash
    the dishes.
Maria li fa lavare a lui. / Mary has him wash them.

Special Topics

§12.

The Verb *Piacere*

§12.1 EXPRESSING "TO LIKE"

The verb *piacere* allows you to express what you like in Italian. But it is a tricky verb because it really means "to be pleasing to."

Tip	When saying that you or someone else likes something, translate the English expression into your mind as "to be pleasing to" and then follow the word order in the formula below.

EXPRESSION	TRANSLATE MENTALLY TO . . .	ITALIAN EXPRESSION
I like that book	"To me is pleasing that book"	*Mi piace quel libro*
We like those books	"To us are pleasing those books"	*Ci piacciono quei libri*

§12.2 CHARACTERISTICS

Piacere is conjugated irregularly in several tenses. You will find
its conjugation in the *Verb Charts* section at the back of this
book.

As mentioned in the *Tip* above, in order to use this verb
correctly, you must always think of what it really means:

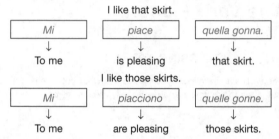

I like that skirt.

Mi	*piace*	*quella gonna.*
↓	↓	↓
To me	is pleasing	that skirt.

I like those skirts.

Mi	*piacciono*	*quelle gonne.*
↓	↓	↓
To me	are pleasing	those skirts.

If you think this way, you will always be correct. Notice that
the real subject is usually put at the end (although this is not
necessary).

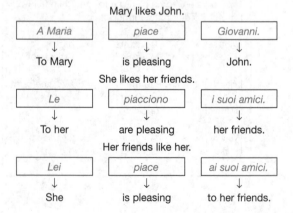

Mary likes John.

A Maria	*piace*	*Giovanni.*
↓	↓	↓
To Mary	is pleasing	John.

She likes her friends.

Le	*piacciono*	*i suoi amici.*
↓	↓	↓
To her	are pleasing	her friends.

Her friends like her.

Lei	*piace*	*ai suoi amici.*
↓	↓	↓
She	is pleasing	to her friends.

Who likes it?

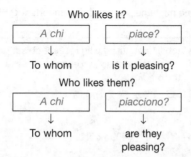

A chi	*piace?*
↓	↓
To whom	is it pleasing?

Who likes them?

A chi	*piacciono?*
↓	↓
To whom	are they pleasing?

In compound tenses (see §8.2-2), *piacere* is conjugated with *essere* (to be). This means, of course, that the past participle agrees with the subject—no matter where it occurs in the sentence.

I didn't like her.

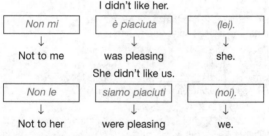

Non mi	*è piaciuta*	*(lei).*
↓	↓	↓
Not to me	was pleasing	she.

She didn't like us.

Non le	*siamo piaciuti*	*(noi).*
↓	↓	↓
Not to her	were pleasing	we.

And do not forget that you might need to use those object pronouns that come after the verb for reasons of emphasis or clarity.

> *La musica piace a me, non a te!* / I like the music, not you
> (The music is pleasing to me, not to you)!

§12.3   A HANDY RULE OF THUMB

As you can see, *piacere* can be very confusing for anyone accustomed to the English verb "to like." The following rule of thumb might help you use this important verb more readily.

Since the verb is often used with indirect object pronouns, just think of the pronouns as *subjects;* then make the verb agree with the *predicate.*

Mi	*piace*	*quella*	*rivista.*
↓	↓	↓	↓
I	like	that	magazine.

(That magazine is pleasing to me.)

Ti	*piacciono*	*quelle*	*riviste.*
↓	↓	↓	↓
You	like	those	magazines.

(Those magazines are pleasing to you.)

Gli	*piace*	*quella*	*rivista.*
↓	↓	↓	↓
He	likes	that	magazine.

(That magazine is pleasing to him.)

Le	*piacciono*	*quelle*	*riviste.*
↓	↓	↓	↓
She	likes	those	magazines.

(Those magazines are pleasing to her.)

Ci	*piace*	*la*	*frutta.*
↓	↓	↓	↓
We	like	(the)	fruit.

(Fruit is pleasing to us.)

Vi	*piacciono*	*i*	*formaggi italiani.*
↓	↓	↓	↓
You	like	(the)	Italian cheeses.

(Italian cheeses are pleasing to you.)

Gli	*piace*	*la*	*verdura.*
↓	↓	↓	↓
They	like	(the)	vegetables.

(Vegetables are pleasing to them.)

Remember: this is merely a rule of thumb. If you are unsure, you must go through the procedure described in §12.2.

§12.4 EXPRESSING "DISLIKE"

To say that you do not like something, simply put *non* before the predicate in the normal fashion (see §2.2-2).

Examples

Non mi piace quella rivista. / I do not like that magazine.
Non le piacciono i ravioli. / She doesn't like ravioli.

Be careful! The verb *dispiacere* is not used to express the same thing. This verb is used in the following ways:

Examples

Mi dispiace. / I'm sorry.
Ti dispiace. / You are sorry.
Gli dispiace. / He is sorry.

§13.
Idiomatic Expressions

§13.1 WHAT ARE IDIOMATIC EXPRESSIONS?

> *Espressioni idiomatiche*

An idiomatic expression is a phrase that is fixed in form and whose meaning cannot always be determined by the meanings of the separate words in it. For example, the English expression *He kicked the bucket* cannot be understood as the sum of the meanings of the separate words. Moreover, it cannot be altered in any way, otherwise it would lose its idiomatic meaning (*He kicks the buckets; He kicks a bucket;* etc.).

§13.2 EXPRESSIONS WITH *AVERE*

The following expressions are made up of *avere* + noun, contrasting with their English equivalents.

> *Ho fame.* / I am hungry (literally: "I have hunger").
> *Non ha paura.* / He is not afraid (literally: "He does not have fear").

EXPRESSIONS WITH *AVERE*	
avercela con qualcuno	to be angry with someone
avere bisogno (di)	to need
avere caldo	to be hot
avere fame	to be hungry
avere freddo	to be cold
avere fretta	to be in a hurry
avere l'occasione di	to have the opportunity to
avere paura	to be afraid

avere ragione	to be right
avere sete	to be thirsty
avere sonno	to be sleepy
avere torto	to be wrong
avere vergogna	to be ashamed
avere voglia (di)	to feel like

Examples

Ieri avevamo fame e abbiamo mangiato molto. / Yesterday we were hungry, so we ate a lot.

Scusa, ma ho fretta. / Excuse me, but I'm in a hurry.

Penso che tu abbia torto. / I believe you are wrong.

Stasera non ho voglia di uscire. / Tonight, I don't feel like going out.

Gli studenti hanno bisogno di tanta pazienza. / The students need a lot of patience.

Perché ce l'hai con Franca? / Why are you angry with Franca?

Tip

When using *molto, tanto* or *poco* with such expressions make sure you treat them as adjectives. They must agree with the gender of noun:

Ho molta fame. / I am very hungry (*la fame* = feminine).

Hanno tanto sonno. / They are very sleepy (*il sonno* = masculine).

Abbiamo poca voglia di uscire. / We have little desire to go out (*la voglia* = feminine).

§13.3 EXPRESSIONS WITH *FARE*, *DARE*, AND *STARE*

If you have forgotten how to conjugate these irregular verbs, just look them up in the *Verb Charts* section at the back of this book.

EXPRESSIONS WITH *FARE*	
fare a meno	to do without
fare attenzione	to pay attention to
fare finta di	to pretend
fare il biglietto	to buy a (transportation) ticket
fare senza	to do without
fare una domanda a	to ask a question
fare una passeggiata	to go for a walk
farsi la barba	to shave
farsi vivo	to show up
Faccia pure!	Go ahead! (Please do!)
Faccio io!	I'll do it!
Non fa niente!	It doesn't matter!
Non fa per me.	It doesn't suit me.

Examples

Ho fatto il biglietto con Alitalia. / I bought my ticket with Alitalia.
Ogni mattina mi faccio la barba. / I shave every morning.
Giovanni, perché non ti fai mai vivo? / John, why don't you come
more often?

EXPRESSIONS WITH *DARE*	
dare fastidio a	to bother (someone)
dare la mano	to shake hands
dare retta a	to heed (pay attention to)
darsi da fare	to get busy

Examples

Il fumo mi dà fastidio. / Smoke bothers me.
Dare la mano a qualcuno è un segno di cortesia. / Shaking
someone's hand is a sign of courtesy.
Da' retta a me! / Heed what I say!

EXPRESSIONS WITH *STARE*	
stare a qualcuno	to be up to someone
stare per	to be about to
stare zitto	to be quiet
Come sta? (pol.)	How are you?
Come stai? (fam.)	How are you?
Sto bene.	I am well.

Examples

Giorgio, sta' zitto! / George, be quiet!
Sta alla signora Rossi scrivere. / It's up to Mrs. Rossi to write.
Ieri stavo per uscire, quando sono arrivati alcuni amici. /
    Yesterday I was about to go out, when some friends arrived.

§13.4 MISCELLANEOUS EXPRESSIONS

a destra	to the right
a sinistra	to the left
nord	north
sud	south
est	east
ovest	west
Ti piace? Altro che!	Do you like it? I'll say!
a lungo andare	in the long run
valere la pena	to be worthwhile
Auguri!	All the best! / Congratulations!
in ogni caso	in any case
Che guaio!	What a mess (to be in)!
Non ne posso più!	I can't stand it anymore!
prendere in giro	to pull one's leg
Ci vuole molto tempo!	It takes a long time!
Lo ha fatto apposta!	He did it on purpose!
Che combinazione!	What a coincidence!

dipendere da	to depend on
qualcosa di buono	something good
niente di buono	nothing good

Examples

Quel negozio si trova a destra. / That store is to the right.
Davvero? Non mi prendere in giro! / Really? Don't pull my leg!
Tutto dipende da te. / Everything depends on you.

§14.
Numbers

§14.1 WHAT ARE CARDINAL AND ORDINAL NUMBERS?

> *I numeri cardinali e ordinali*

Cardinal numbers are used for counting (*one*, *two*, *three*, etc.). *Ordinal numbers* are used to indicate order *(first, second, third,* etc.).

§14.2 CARDINAL NUMBERS

ZERO TO TWENTY			
0	zero	11	undici
1	uno	12	dodici
2	due	13	tredici
3	tre	14	quattordici
4	quattro	15	quindici
5	cinque	16	sedici
6	sei	17	diciassette
7	sette	18	diciotto
8	otto	19	diciannove
9	nove	20	venti
10	dieci		

The numbers from twenty on are formed by adding the first nine numbers to each new category of tens, keeping the following adjustments in mind:

In front of *uno* and *otto* (the two numbers that start with a vowel), drop the final vowel of the tens number:

| 21 | *venti* | → | *vent-* + *uno* | → | *ventuno* |
| 38 | *trenta* | → | *trent-* + *otto* | → | *trentotto* |

When *tre* is added on, it must be written with an accent (to show that the stress is on the final vowel):

| 23 | *venti* + *tre* | → | *ventitrè* |
| 33 | *trenta* + *tre* | → | *trenatrè* |

TWENTY TO ONE HUNDRED			
20	*venti*	60	*sessanta*
21	*ventuno*	61	*sessantuno*
22	*ventidue*	62	*sessantadue*
23	*ventitrè*	63	*sessantatrè*
24	*ventiquattro*	. . .	
25	*venticinque*	70	*settanta*
26	*ventisei*	71	*settantuno*
27	*ventisette*	72	*settantadue*
28	*ventotto*	73	*settantatrè*
29	*ventinove*	. . .	
30	*trenta*	80	*ottanta*
31	*trentuno*	81	*ottantuno*
32	*trentadue*	82	*ottantadue*
. . .		83	*ottantatrè*
40	*quaranta*	. . .	
41	*quarantuno*	90	*novanta*
42	*quarantadue*	91	*novantuno*
43	*quarantatrè*	92	*novantadue*
. . .		93	*novantatrè*
50	*cinquanta*	94	*novantaquattro*

TWENTY TO ONE HUNDRED			
51	*cinquantuno*	95	*novantacinque*
52	*cinquantadue*	96	*novantasei*
53	*cinquantatrè*	. . .	
. . .		100	*cento*

The same method of construction applies to the remaining numbers:

NUMBERS ABOVE ONE HUNDRED			
101	*centuno*	2000	*duemila*
102	*centodue*	3000	*tremila*
. . .		. . .	
200	*duecento*	100.000	*centomila*
300	*trecento*	200.000	*duecentomila*
. . .		. . .	
900	*novecento*	1.000.000	*un milione*
. . .		2.000.000	*due milioni*
1000	*mille*	3.000.000	*tre milioni*
1001	*milleuno*	. . .	
1002	*milledue*	1.000.000.000	*un miliardo*

Notice that the plural of *mille* is *mila*, whereas *un milione* and *un miliardo* are pluralized in the normal way (§3.3-1).

Examples

due milioni / two million
tre miliardi / three billion

Cardinal numbers normally are placed before a noun.

Examples

tre persone / three persons
cinquantotto minuti / fifty-eight minutes

When you put *uno* (or any number constructed with it,
e.g., *ventuno*, *trentuno*, etc.), then you must treat it exactly
like the indefinite article (see §4.2–2).

uno zio / one uncle
ventun anni / twenty-one years

Milione and *miliardo* are always followed by *di* before a noun.

Examples

un milione di dollari / a million dollars
due milioni di abitanti / two million inhabitants
tre miliardi di lire / three billion liras

The cardinal numbers may be written as one word. But for
large numbers, it is better to separate them logically, so that
they can be read easily.

30.256 = *trentamila duecento cinquantasei* (rather than
trentamiladuecentocinquantasei!)

§14.3 ORDINAL NUMBERS

First to tenth			
1st	*primo*	6th	*sesto*
2nd	*secondo*	7th	*settimo*
3rd	*terzo*	8th	*ottavo*
4th	*quarto*	9th	*nono*
5th	*quinto*	10th	*decimo*

The remaining numerals are easily constructed in the following
manner.

Take the corresponding cardinal number, drop its vowel ending, and then add *-esimo*

11th	undici	→	undic- + -esimo
		→	undicesimo
42nd	quarantadue	→	quarantadu + -esimo
		→	quarantaduesimo

In the case of numbers ending in *-trè*, remove the accent mark, but keep the final *-e*.

| 23rd | ventitrè + -esimo | → | ventitreesimo |
| 33rd | trentatrè + -esimo | → | trentatreesimo |

Unlike the cardinal numbers, ordinals are adjectives that precede the noun. Therefore, they agree with the noun in the normal fashion (see §6.2).

Examples

il primo giorno / the first day
la ventesima volta / the twentieth time
gli ottavi capitoli / the eighth chapters

As any adjective, the ordinals can be easily transformed into pronouns (see §7.2).

È il terzo in fila. / He is the third in line.

As in English, ordinals are used to express the denominator of fractions, whereas the numerator is expressed by cardinals.

tre quarti   *un diciassettesimo*

| 3 | → | tre | | 1 | → | un |
| 4 | → | quarti (pl.) | | 17 | → | diciassettesimo (sing.) |

> **Be careful!**
>
> 1/2 = *mezzo*/*metà*
>
> *mezzo litro* / a half liter
> *la metà di tutto* / half of everything

The definite article is not used with a proper name.

Examples

Papa Giovanni XXIII (= *ventitreesimo*) / Pope John (the) XXIII
Luigi XIV (= *quattordicesimo*) / Louis (the) XIV

§14.4 NUMERICAL EXPRESSIONS

L'ARITMETICA / **ARITHMETIC**
L'addizione / Addition
23 + 36 = 59   *ventitrè più trantasei fa (uguale) cinquantanove*
La sottrazione / Subtraction
8 − 3 = 5   *otto meno tre fa (uguale) cinque*
La moltiplicazione / Multiplication
7 × 2 = 14   *sette per due fa (uguale) quattordici*
La divisione / Division
16 ÷ 2 = 8   *Sedici diviso per due fa (uguale) otto*

AGE

Quanti anni ha (pol.)?	How old are you?
Quanti anni hai (fam.)?	How old are you?
Ho ventidue anni.	I am twenty-two years old (literally: "I have 22 years").
Ho trentanove anni.	I am thirty-nine years old (literally: "I have 39 years").

A FEW USEFUL EXPRESSIONS

il doppio	double
a due a due, a tre a tre, . . .	two by two, three by three, . . .
una dozzina	a dozen
una ventina, una trentina, . . .	about twenty, about thirty, . . .
un centinaio, due centinaia, tre centinaia, . . .	about a hundred, about two hundred, about three hundred, . . .
un migliaio, due migliaia, tre migliaia, . . .	about a thousand, about two thousand, about three thousand, . . .

§15.
Telling Time

§15.1 WHAT TIME IS IT?

> *Che ora è?*

You can ask the question of "What time is it?" in the singular:

Che ora è?

Or in the plural:

Che ore sono?

The word *ora* literally means "hour." The abstract concept of "time" is expressed by *il tempo*.

Come passa il tempo! / How time flies!

§15.2 HOURS

> *Le ore*

The hours are feminine. Therefore, they are preceded by the feminine forms of the definite article (see §4.2–1):

Examples

l'una / one o'clock (= the only singular form)
le due / two o'clock
le tre / three o'clock
le quattro / four o'clock

Do not forget to make your verbs and prepositions agree!

È l'una.	It's one o'clock.
Sono le due.	It's two o'clock.
Sono le tre.	It's three o'clock.
A che ora arriverai?	At what time are you arriving?
All'una.	At one o'clock.
Alle due.	At two o'clock.
Alle tre.	At three o'clock.

In ordinary conversation, morning, afternoon, and evening hours are distinguished by the following expressions:

di mattina (della mattina)	in the morning
di pomeriggio	in the afternoon
di sera (della sera)	in the evening
di notte (della notte)	in the night/at night

Examples

Sono le otto di mattina. / It's eight o'clock in the morning.
Sono le nove di sera. / It's nine o'clock in the evening.

Although *pomeriggio* means "afternoon," in some parts of Italy *sera* is sometimes used to refer to P.M.

Officially, telling time in Italian is on the basis of the twenty-four hour clock. Thus, after the noon hour (*le dodici*), official hours are as follows:

Examples

Sono le quindici. / It's 3 P.M.
Sono le venti. / It's 8 P.M.
Sono le ventiquattro. / It's (twelve) midnight.

§15.3 MINUTES

I minuti

Minutes are simply added to the hour with the conjunction *e* (and).

Examples

Sono le tre e venti. / It's three-twenty.
Sono le quattro e dieci. / It's ten after four.
È l'una e quaranta. / It's one-forty.
Sono le sedici e cinquanta. / It's 4:50 P.M.
Sono le ventidue e cinque. / It's 10:05 P.M.

As the next hour approaches, an alternative way of expressing the minutes is: the next hour minus (*meno*) the number of minutes left to go.

8:58 = *le otto e cinquantotto* or *le nove meno due*
10:50 = *le dieci e cinquanta* or *le undici meno dieci*

The expressions *un quarto* (a quarter), and *mezzo/mezza* (half) can be used for the quarter and half hour.

3:15 = *le tre e quindici* or *le tre e un quarto*
4:30 = *le quattro e trenta* or *le quattro e mezzo/mezza*
5:45 = *le cinque e quarantacinque* or *le sei meno un quarto* or *le cinque e tre quarti* (three quarters)

§15.4 TIME EXPRESSIONS

le dodici or *mezzogiorno*	noon/midday
le ventiquattro or *mezzanotte*	midnight
È mezzogiorno e un quarto.	It's a quarter past noon.
È mezzanotte e mezzo.	It's half past midnight.
il secondo	second
l'orologio	watch, clock
L'orologio va avanti.	The watch is fast.
L'orologio va indietro.	The watch is slow.
il quadrante	dial
la lancetta	hand (of a clock)
l'orario	schedule
preciso	exactly
È l'una precisa.	It's exactly one o'clock.
Sono le tre e mezzo precise.	It's three-thirty exactly.
in punto	on the dot
È l'una in punto.	It's one o'clock on the dot.
Sono le tre e mezzo in punto.	It's three-thirty on the dot.

§16.
Days, Months, Seasons, Dates, and Weather

§16.1   WHAT'S TODAY'S DATE?

> *Che giorno è oggi?*

In addition to *Che giorno è?* (literally "What day is it?"), the following expression is also used.

> *Quanti ne abbiamo oggi?* / (literally) How many of them
>   (= days of the month) do we have today?
> *Ne abbiamo quindici.* / It's the fifteenth.

If you want to find out the complete date (day, month, and if needed, year), then you would ask:

> *Che data è?* / What date is it?
> *È il ventuno settembre.* / It's September twenty-first.

Tip	As a rule of thumb, use *Che giorno è?* unless you want specific information on the month or year.

§16.2   DAYS OF THE WEEK

> *I giorni della settimana*

lunedì	Monday
martedì	Tuesday
mercoledì	Wednesday
giovedì	Thursday
venerdì	Friday
sabato	Saturday
domenica	Sunday

The formula "On Mondays, Tuesdays," etc. is rendered in Italian with the definite article. Note that the days are masculine, except for *domenica,* which is feminine.

Examples

il martedì / On Mondays
il sabato / On Saturdays
la domenica / On Sundays

Notice that the days are not capitalized (unless, of course, they are the first word of a sentence).

§16.3 MONTHS OF THE YEAR

I mesi dell'anno

gennaio	January
febbraio	February
marzo	March
aprile	April
maggio	May
giugno	June
luglio	July
agosto	August
settembre	September
ottobre	October
novembre	November
dicembre	December

Notice that the months are not capitalized (unless, of course, they are the first word of a sentence).

The preposition *di* is often used with a month to indicate something habitual or permanent.

Examples

Di febbraio andiamo spesso al mare. / Every February we often go to the sea.
Di maggio c'è sempre tanto sole. / In May there is always lots of sunshine.

The preposition *a* is used to indicate when something will take place.

Examples

Verrò a giugno. / I will come in May.
Torneranno a luglio. / They will return in July.

The preposition *tra (fra)* is used to convey "in how much time" something will be done.

Examples

Maria andrà in Italia tra due mesi. / Mary is going to Italy in two months time.
Arriveremo fra otto ore. / We will arrive in eight hours' time.

§16.4 SEASONS

Le stagioni

la primavera	spring
l'estate	summer
l'autunno	fall
l'inverno	winter

§16.5   RELATED EXPRESSIONS

prossimo (-a)	next
la settimana prossima	next week
il mese prossimo	next month
scorso (-a)	last
la settimana scorsa	last week
il mese scorso	last month
a domani, a giovedì, etc.	till tomorrow, till Thursday, etc.
domani a otto, domenica a otto, etc.	a week from tomorrow, a week from Sunday, etc.
il giorno	the day
la giornata	the whole day (long)
la sera	the evening
la serata	the whole evening (long)
oggi	today
ieri	yesterday
domani	tomorrow
avantieri	the day before yesterday
dopodomani	the day after tomorrow

§16.6   DATES

la data

Dates are expressed by the following formula:

Masculine definite article	Cardinal number	Month
↓	↓	↓
il	*tre*	*maggio*
il	*quattro*	*aprile*
il	*ventitrè*	*giugno*
il	*ventuno*	*settembre*

Examples

Oggi è il ventinove gennaio. / Today is January 29.
Oggi è il quindici settembre. / Today is September 15.
Oggi è lunedì, il sedici marzo. / Today is Monday, March 16.
Oggi è mercoledì, il quattro dicembre. / Today is Wednesday, December 4.

The exception to this formula is the first day of every month, for which you must use the ordinal number *primo*.

Examples

È il primo ottobre. / It's October 1.
È il primo giugno. / It's June 1.

Years are always preceded by the definite article.

Examples

È il 2004. / It's 2004.
Sono nato nel 1972. / I was born in 1972.
  ⌃
 in + il

However, in complete dates, the article is omitted before the year.

Oggi è il cinque febbraio, 2005. / Today is February 5, 2005.

§16.7 THE WEATHER

| Il tempo |

Che tempo fa?	How's the weather?
Fa bel tempo.	It's beautiful (weather).
Fa brutto (cattivo) tempo.	It's bad (awful) weather.
Fa caldo.	It's hot.
Fa freddo.	It's cold.
Fa molto caldo (freddo).	It's very hot (cold).
Fa un po' caldo (freddo).	It's a bit hot (cold).
Fa fresco.	It's cool.
Il caldo (freddo) è insopportabile.	The heat (cold) is unbearable.

Le previsioni del tempo	The weather forecast
Piove.	It is raining.
Nevica.	It is snowing.
Tira vento.	It is windy.
È nuvoloso.	It is cloudy.
la pioggia	rain
la neve	snow
il vento	wind
la grandine	hail
l'alba	dawn
il tramonto	twilight
il temporale	storm
il tuono (verb: *tuonare*)	clap of thunder
il lampo (verb: *lampeggiare*)	flash of lightning

Use the appropriate verb tense when referring to the weather in the past or the future.

Examples

Ieri pioveva. / It was raining yesterday.

Domani nevicherà. / Tomorrow it will snow.

La settimana scorsa faceva molto freddo. / It was very cold last week.

Quest'anno ha fatto bel tempo. / This year the weather has been beautiful.

When referring to climate conditions in general, use *essere* instead of *fare*:

Examples

In Sicilia l'inverno è sempre bello. / Winter is always beautiful in Sicily.

L'estate è fresca in Piemonte. / Summer is cool in Piedmont.

§17.

Common Conversation Techniques

§17.1   WHAT IS A CONVERSATION?

La conversazione

A *conversation* is a spoken exchange of thoughts, opinions, and feelings. Knowing how to converse involves knowing which words, phrases, expressions, and types of sentence apply to a given situation.

By knowing grammar, you already know quite a bit about how to converse—for instance, you'll need interrogative adjectives to ask questions; imperative verb forms to give commands; subjunctive tenses to express opinion, doubt, wishes, etc. However, there are some aspects of communication that are purely formulaic or idiomatic. The following are a few common formulas that occur frequently in conversations.

§17.2 STARTING AND ENDING CONVERSATIONS

SAYING HELLO/RESPONDING IN POLITE SPEECH	
Buon giorno, signor Verdi, come va?	Hello/Good morning, Mr. Verdi, how's it going?
Bene, grazie, e Lei?	Well, thanks, and you?
Buon pomeriggio, signora Verdi, come sta?	Hello/Good afternoon, Mrs. Verdi, how are you?
Non c'è male, grazie.	Not bad, thanks.
Buona sera, signora Rossi, come sta?	Hello/Good evening, Mrs. Rossi, how are you?
Abbastanza bene, grazie, e Lei?	Quite well, thanks, and you?

SAYING HELLO/RESPONDING IN INFORMAL SPEECH	
Ciao, come va?	Hi, how's it going?
Benissimo, e tu?	Very well, and you?
Salve, come stai?	Greetings, how are you?
Così, così.	So, so.

ON THE PHONE	
Pronto.	Hello.
Chi parla?	Who's speaking?/Who is it?
Con chi parlo?	With whom am I speaking?
Sono Dino Franceschi.	This is Dino Franceschi.
C'è il signor Marchi?	Is Mr. Marchi there?

ENDING CONVERSATIONS/PHONE CALLS	
Buon giorno!	Have a good day!
Buona serata!	Have a good evening!
ArrivederLa (polite)!	Good-bye!
Arrivederci (familiar)!	Good-bye!
Ciao!	Bye!
A presto!	See you soon!
Ci vediamo!	See you!
A più tardi!	See you later!

In polite address, "hello" is expressed as *buon giorno* (also written as one word *buongiorno*) ("good morning") until noon, as *buon pomeriggio* ("good afternoon") in the afternoon, and *buona sera* (also written as one word *buonasera*) ("good evening") in the evening. In familiar address, *ciao* ("hi") is used at any time of the day.

When approached by waiters, store clerks, etc., you will often hear:

> *Desidera?* (sing.) / *Desiderano?* (pl.)
> May I help you?

§17.3 INTRODUCING PEOPLE

Come si chiama, Lei? (pol.)	What is your name?
Come ti chiami? (fam.)	What's your name?
Mi chiamo Mara Fratti.	My name is Mara Fratti.
Le presento la signora Gentile (pol.).	Allow me to introduce you to Mrs. Gentile.
Ti presento Alessandro Dini (fam.).	Let me introduce you to Alexander Dini.
Piacere di fare la Sua conoscenza (pol.).	A pleasure to make your acquaintance.
Piacere di fare la tua conoscenza (fam.).	A pleasure to make your acquaintance.

§17.4 BEING POLITE

Scusi (pol.).	Excuse me.
Scusi (fam.).	Excuse me.
Permesso.	Excuse me (used when making one's way through people).
Grazie molto.	Thanks a lot.
Grazie mille.	Thanks a million (literally "a thousand")

§17.5 EXPRESSING YOUR FEELINGS

SURPRISE	
Vero?/Davvero?/No!	Really?
Come?	How come?
Scherza (pol.)?/*Scherzi?* (fam.)	Are you kidding?
Incredibile!	Unbelievable!/Incredibile!

AGREEMENT/DISAGREEMENT	
Buon'idea!	Good idea!
D'accordo./Va bene.	OK.
Non va bene.	It's not OK.
Non sono d'accordo.	I don't agree.

PITY/RESIGNATION	
Peccato.	Too bad./It's a pity.
Mi dispiace.	I'm sorry.
Che triste!	How sad!
Non c'è niente da fare.	There's nothing to do.
Pazienza!	Patience!

INDIFFERENCE/BOREDOM	
Non importa.	It doesn't matter.
Per me è lo stesso.	It's all the same to me.
Fa lo stesso.	It's all the same thing to me.
Uffa!	Exclamation similar to "Ugh!"
Basta!	Enough!
Che noia!	What a bore!

§18.
Synonyms and Antonyms

§18.1 WHAT ARE SYNONYMS AND ANTONYMS?

> *I sinonimi e i contrari*

Synonyms are words that have the same meaning. *Antonyms* are words that have an opposite meaning. Being able to relate words as synonyms or antonyms will help you learn and remember vocabulary.

§18.2 SYNONYMS

Synonyms allow you to say the same thing in a different way, thus increasing your communicative competence. Keep in mind, however, that no two words have the exact same meaning in every situation.

ENGLISH MEANING	ITALIAN SYNONYMS	
to ask	*chiedere*	*domandare*
crazy	*pazzo*	*matto*
dress/suit	*l'abito*	*il vestito*
face	*la faccia*	*il viso*
gladly	*volentieri*	*con piacere*
much/many/a lot	*molto*	*tanto*
near	*vicino*	*presso*
nothing	*niente*	*nulla*
now	*ora*	*adesso*
only	*solo*	*solamente, soltanto*
please	*per piacere*	*per favore*

English Meaning	Italian Synonyms	
quick(ly)	*veloce(mente)*	*svelto*
the same	*lo stesso*	*uguale*
slowly	*lentamente*	*piano*
street/road	*la strada*	*la via*
therefore	*quindi*	*dunque, perciò*
truly/really	*veramente*	*davvero*
to understand	*capire*	*comprendere*
unfortunately	*purtroppo*	*sfortunatamente*

The verbs *conoscere* and *sapere* both mean "to know." But they are used in specific ways.

"To know someone" is rendered by *conoscere*.

Examples

Maria non conosce quell'avvocato. / Mary doesn't know that lawyer.
Chi conosce la dottoressa Verdi? / Who knows Dr. Verdi?

"To know how to do something" is rendered by *sapere*.

Examples

Mia sorella non sa pattinare. / My sister doesn't know how too skate.
Sai cucire? / Do you know how to sew?

"To know something" is rendered by *sapere*.

Examples

Marco non sa la verità. / Mark doesn't know the truth.
Chi sa come si chiama quella donna? / Who knows what that
woman's name is?

"To be familiar with something" is rendered by *conoscere*.

Examples

Conosci Roma? / Are you familiar with Rome?
Conosco un bel ristorante qui vicino. / I know a good restaurant
nearby.

When referring to knowledge, *sapere* implies complete
knowledge, *conoscere* partial knowledge.

Examples

Lo sai l'italiano? / Do you know Italian?
Conosco qualche parola. / I know a few words.

Tip

As a rule of thumb, use *conoscere* when referring
to people and *sapere* to things.

Conosco Alessandro. / I know Alexander.
Sanno parlare bene. / They know how to speak
well.

---

§18.3 ANTONYMS

Antonyms allow you to say the opposite or the counterpart of
something. This type of knowledge too will increase your
communicative competence. Keep in mind, however, that no
two words have the exact opposite meaning in every
situation.

l'alba	sunrise	*il tramonto*	sunset
alto	tall	*basso*	short
aperto	open	*chiuso*	closed
l'atterraggio	landing	*il decollo*	take-off
bello	beautiful	*brutto*	ugly
bene	well	*male*	bad
bianco	white	*nero*	black
buono	good	*cattivo*	bad
chiaro	clear	*scuro*	dark
dentro	inside	*fuori*	outside
l'entrata	entrance	*l'uscita*	exit
facile	easy	*difficile*	difficult
magro	thin, skinny	*grasso*	fat
presto	early	*tardi*	late
pulito	clean	*sporco*	dirty
piccolo	small	*grande*	big
primo	first	*ultimo*	last
ricco	rich	*povero*	poor
simpatico	nice, pleasant	*antipatico*	unpleasant
spesso	often	*mai*	never
tanto, molto	much, a lot	*poco*	little, a bit
trovare	to find	*perdere*	to lose
tutto	everything	*niente, nulla*	nothing
vecchio	old	*giovane*	young
vendere	to sell	*comprare*	to buy
venire	to come	*andare*	to go
vicino	near	*lontano*	far
vuoto	empty	*pieno*	full

§19.

Cognates: Good and False Friends

§19.1 WHAT ARE COGNATES?

Another good way to learn and remember vocabulary is to recognize *cognates*. Cognates are Italian words that look very similar to English words. This is because the words are related in origin, having developed from the same ancestral roots. They are, so to speak, "friends." But just like friends, they can be "good" or "false."

§19.2 THE GOOD FRIENDS

Cognates that have the *same* meaning are, of course, good friends. Generally speaking, good friends can be recognized by their endings. Needless to say, you must always be wary of spelling differences!

ENGLISH ENDINGS	COGNATE ITALIAN ENDINGS
-tion	-zione
action	l'azione
admiration	l'ammirazione
attention	l'attenzione
condition	la condizione
conversation	la conversazione
implication	l'implicazione
nation	la nazione
operation	l'operazione

ENGLISH ENDINGS	COGNATE ITALIAN ENDINGS
-sion	-sione
conclusion	la conclusione
delusion	la delusione
occasion	l'occasione
tension	la tensione
-ty	-tà
city	la città
rarity	la rarità
society	la società
university	l'università
-ce	-za
appearance	l'apparenza
difference	la differenza
importance	l'importanza
violence	la violenza
-or	-ore
actor	l'attore
doctor	il dottore
professor	il professore
-ary	-ario
arbitrary	arbitrario
ordinary	ordinario
vocabulary	il vocabolario
-ist	-ista
dentist	il/la dentista
pianist	il/la pianista
tourist	il/la turista
violinist	il/la violinista

ENGLISH ENDINGS	COGNATE ITALIAN ENDINGS
-logy	*-logia*
anthropology	*l'antropologia*
archeology	*l'archeologia*
biology	*la biologia*
psychology	*la psicologia*
zoology	*la zoologia*
-ical	*-ico*
typical	*tipico*
political	*politico*
practical	*pratico*
economical	*economico*
-al	*-ale*
animal	*l'animale*
central	*centrale*
social	*sociale*
special	*speciale*
-ect	*-etto*
correct	*corretto*
direct	*diretto*
perfect	*perfetto*
-ous	*-oso*
famous	*famoso*
generous	*generoso*
-phy	*-fia*
geography	*la geografia*
philosophy	*la filosofia*
photography	*la fotografia*
-ly	*-mente*
rarely	*raramente*
correctly	*correttamente*

But be careful! These patterns do not always hold.

ENGLISH WORDS	EQUIVALENT ITALIAN WORDS WITH DIFFERENT ENDINGS
amity	*l'amicizia*
beauty	*la bellezza (beltà)*
civilization	*la civiltà*

Of course you will also find many good friends among the verbs.

ENGLISH VERBS	COGNATE ITALIAN VERBS
(to) analyze	*analizzare*
(to) complicate	*complicare*
(to) emigrate	*emigrare*
(to) indicate	*indicare*
(to) prefer	*preferire*

§19.3 THE FALSE FRIENDS

Cognates with different meanings are, needless to say, false friends. Here are a few very common ones:

ENGLISH WORD	FALSE FRIEND	CORRECT WORD
accident	*l'accidente* = unexpected event	*l'incidente*
argument	*l'argomento* = topic (of discussion)	*la discussione, la lite*
assist	*assistere* = to be present	*aiutare*

English Word	False Friend	Correct Word
brave	*bravo* = good	*coraggioso*
complexion	*la complessione* = build, physique	*la carnagione*
conductor (musical)	*il conduttore* = bus/train conductor	*il direttore*
confront	*confrontare* = to compare	*affrontare*
contest	*il contesto* = context	*il concorso*
disgrace	*la disgrazia* = misfortune	*la vergogna*
effective	*effettivo* = actual	*efficace*
factory	*la fattoria* = farm	*la fabbrica*
firm	*la firma* = signature	*la ditta, l'azienda*
large	*largo* = wide	*grande*
lecture	*la lettura* = reading	*la conferenza*
magazine	*il magazzino* = warehouse, department store	*la rivista*
sensible	*sensibile* = sensitive	*sensato*
stamp	*la stampa* = the press	*il francobollo*

Tip

Do not assume that cognates have the exact same meanings. Even among the good friends, sometimes the meanings are not identical. For example, the cognates *finally* and *finalmente* mean "finally," but only in the sense of "at last."

It is always wise to keep a good dictionary on hand to check for differences in meaning or usage!

Verb Charts

The following verbs are irregular in one or more tenses as shown.

(* = conjugated with *essere* in compound tenses)

andare * / to go

Present Indicative	(io) vado, (tu) vai, (Lei) va, (lui / lei) va, (noi) andiamo, (voi) andate, (loro) vanno
Future	(io) andrò, (tu) andrai, (Lei) andrà, (lui / lei) andrà, (noi) andremo, (voi) andrete, (loro) andranno
Imperative	(tu) va', (Lei) vada, (noi) andiamo, (voi) andate, (Loro) vadano
Conditional	(io) andrei, (tu) andresti, (Lei) andrebbe, (lui / lei) andrebbe, (noi) andremmo, (voi) andreste, (loro) andrebbero
Present Subjunctive	(io) vada (tu) vada, (Lei) vada, (lui / lei) vada, (noi) andiamo, (voi) andiate, (loro) vadano

aprire / to open

Past Participle	aperto

avere / to have

Present Indicative	(io) ho, (tu) hai, (Lei) ha, (lui / lei) ha, (noi) abbiamo, (voi) avete, (loro) hanno
Past Absolute	(io) ebbi, (tu) avesti, (Lei) ebbe, (lui / lei) ebbe, (noi) avemmo, (voi) aveste, (loro) ebbero
Future	(io) avrò, (tu) avrai, (Lei) avrà, (lui / lei) avrà, (noi) avremo, (voi) avrete, (loro) avranno
Imperative	(tu) abbi, (Lei) abbia, (noi) abbiamo, (voi) abbiate, (Loro) abbiano

242

Conditional	(io) avrei, (tu) avresti, (Lei) avrebbe, (lui / lei) avrebbe, (noi) avremmo, (voi) avreste, (loro) avrebbero
Present Subjunctive	(io) abbia (tu) abbia, (Lei) abbia, (lui / lei) abbia, (noi) abbiamo, (voi) abbiate, (loro) abbiano

<u>bere</u> / to drink

Present Indicative	(io) bevo, (tu) bevi, (Lei) beve, (lui / lei) beve, (noi) beviamo, (voi) bevete, (loro) bevono
Past Participle	bevuto
Imperfect	(io) bevevo, (tu) bevevi, (Lei) beveva, (lui / lei) beveva, (noi) bevevamo, (voi) bevevate, (loro) bevevano
Past Absolute	(io) bevvi (bevetti), (tu) bevesti, (Lei) bevve (bevette), (lui / lei) bevve (bevette), (noi) bevemmo, (voi) beveste, (loro) bevvero (bevettero)
Future	(io) berrò, (tu) berrai, (Lei) berrà, (lui / lei) berrà, (noi) berremo, (voi) berrete, (loro) berranno
Imperative	(tu) bevi, (Lei) beva, (noi) beviamo, (voi) bevete, (Loro) bevano
Conditional	(io) berrei, (tu) berresti, (Lei) berrebbe, (lui / lei) berrebbe, (noi) berremmo, (voi) berreste, (loro) berrebbero
Present Subjunctive	(io) beva, (tu) beva, (Lei) beva, (lui / lei) beva, (noi) beviamo, (voi) beviate, (loro) bevano
Gerund	bevendo

<u>cadere</u>* / to fall

Past Absolute	(io) caddi, (tu) cadesti, (Lei) cadde, (lui / lei) cadde, (noi) cademmo, (voi) cadeste, (loro) caddero

Future	(io) cadrò, (tu) cadrai, (Lei) cadrà, (lui / lei) cadrà, (noi) cadremo, (voi) cadrete, (loro) cadranno
Conditional	(io) cadrei, (tu) cadresti, (Lei) cadrebbe, (lui / lei) cadrebbe, (noi) cadremmo, (voi) cadreste, (loro) cadrebbero
Present Subjunctive	(io) cada, (tu) cada, (Lei) cada, (lui / lei) cada, (noi) cadiamo, (voi) cadiate, (loro) cadano

chiedere / to ask for

Past Participle	chiesto
Past Absolute	(io) chiesi, (tu) chiedesti, (Lei) chiese, (lui / lei) chiese, (noi) chiedemmo, (voi) chiedeste, (loro) chiesero

chiudere / to close

Past Participle	chiuso
Past Absolute	(io) chiusi, (tu) chiudesti, (Lei) chiuse, (lui / lei) chiuse, (noi) chiudemmo, (voi) chiudeste, (loro) chiusero

conoscere / to know

Past Absolute	(io) conobbi, (tu) conoscesti, (Lei) conobbe, (lui / lei) conobbe, (noi) conoscemmo, (voi) conosceste, (loro) conobbero

dare / to give

Present Indicative	(io) do, (tu) dai, (Lei) dà, (lui / lei) dà, (noi) diamo, (voi) date, (loro) danno
Past Participle	dato
Imperfect	(io) davo, (tu) davi, (Lei) dava, (lui / lei) dava, (noi) davamo, (voi) davate, (loro) davano
Past Absolute	(io) diedi, (tu) desti, (Lei) diede, (lui / lei) diede, (noi) demmo, (voi) deste, (loro) diedero

Future	(io) darò, (tu) darai, (Lei) darà, (lui / lei) darà, (noi) daremo, (voi) darete, (loro) daranno
Imperative	(tu) da', (Lei) dia, (noi) diamo, (voi) date, (Loro) diano
Present Subjunctive	(io) dia, (tu) dia, (Lei) dia, (lui / lei) dia, (noi) diamo, (voi) diate, (loro) diano
Imperfect Subjunctive	(io) dessi, (tu) dessi, (Lei) desse, (lui / lei) desse, (noi) dessimo, (voi) deste, (loro) dessero
Gerund	dando

decidere/ to decide

Past Participle	deciso
Past Absolute	(io) decisi, (tu) decidesti, (Lei) decise, (lui / lei) decise, (noi) decidemmo, (voi) decideste, (loro) decisero

dire/ to say, tell

Present Indicative	(io) dico, (tu) dici, (Lei) dice, (lui / lei) dice, (noi) diciamo, (voi) dite, (loro) dicono
Past Participle	detto
Imperfect	(io) dicevo, (tu) dicevi, (Lei) diceva, (lui / lei) diceva, (noi) dicevamo, (voi) dicevate, (loro) dicevano
Past Absolute	(io) dissi, (tu) dicesti, (Lei) disse, (lui / lei) disse, (noi) dicemmo, (voi) diceste, (loro) dissero
Future	(io) dirò, (tu) dirai, (Lei) dirà, (lui / lei) dirà, (noi) diremo, (voi) direte, (loro) diranno
Imperative	(tu) di', (Lei) dica, (noi) diciamo, (voi) dite, (Loro) dicano
Conditional	(io) direi, (tu) diresti, (Lei) direbbe, (lui / lei) direbbe, (noi) diremmo, (voi) direste, (loro) direbbero

Present Subjunctive	(io) dica, (tu) dica, (Lei) dica, (lui / lei) dica, (noi) diciamo, (voi) diciate, (loro) dicano
Imperfect Subjunctive	(io) dicessi, (tu) dicessi, (Lei) dicesse, (lui / lei) dicesse, (noi) dicessimo, (voi) diceste, (loro) dicessero
Gerund	dicendo

<u>dovere</u> / to have to

Present Indicative	(io) devo, (tu) devi, (Lei) deve, (lui / lei) deve, (noi) dobbiamo, (voi) dovete, (loro) devono
Future	(io) dovrò, (tu) dovrai, (Lei) dovrà, (lui / lei) dovrà, (noi) dovremo, (voi) dovrete, (loro) dovranno
Conditional	(io) dovrei, (tu) dovresti, (Lei) dovrebbe, (lui / lei) dovrebbe, (noi) dovremmo, (voi) dovreste, (loro) dovrebbero
Present Subjunctive	(io) deva (debba), (tu) deva (debba), (Lei) deva (debba), (lui / lei) deve, (noi) dobbiamo, (voi) dobbiate, (loro) devano (debbano)

<u>essere</u>* / to be

Present Indicative	(io) sono, (tu) sei, (Lei) è, (lui / lei) è, (noi) siamo, (voi) siete, (loro) sono
Past Participle	stato
Imperfect	(io) ero, (tu) eri, (Lei) era, (lui / lei) era, (noi) eravamo, (voi) eravate, (loro) erano
Past Absolute	(io) fui, (tu) fosti, (Lei) fu, (lui / lei) fu, (noi) fummo, (voi) foste, (loro) furono
Future	(io) sarò, (tu) sarai, (Lei) sarà, (lui / lei) sarà, (noi) saremo, (voi) sarete, (loro) saranno
Imperative	(tu) sii, (Lei) sia, (noi) siamo, (voi) siate, (Loro) siano

Conditional	(io) sarei, (tu) saresti, (Lei) sarebbe, (lui / lei) sarebbe, (noi) saremmo, (voi) sareste, (loro) sarebbero
Present Subjunctive	(io) sia, (tu) sia, (Lei) sia, (lui / lei) sia, (noi) siamo, (voi) siate, (loro) siano
Imperfect Subjunctive	(io) fossi, (tu) fossi, (Lei) fosse, (lui / lei) fosse, (noi) fossimo, (voi) foste, (loro) fossero

<u>*fare*</u> / to do, make

Present Indicative	(io) faccio, (tu) fai, (Lei) fa, (lui / lei) fa, (noi) facciamo, (voi) fate, (loro) fanno
Past Participle	fatto
Imperfect	(io) facevo, (tu) facevi, (Lei) faceva, (lui / lei) faceva, (noi) facevamo, (voi) facevate, (loro) facevano
Past Absolute	(io) feci, (tu) facesti, (Lei) fece, (lui / lei) fece, (noi) facemmo, (voi) faceste, (loro) fecero
Future	(io) farò, (tu) farai, (Lei) farà, (lui / lei) farà, (noi) faremo, (voi) farete, (loro) faranno
Imperative	(tu) fa', (Lei) faccia, (noi) facciamo, (voi) fate, (Loro) facciano
Conditional	(io) farei, (tu) faresti, (Lei) farebbe, (lui / lei) farebbe, (noi) faremmo, (voi) fareste, (loro) farebbero
Present Subjunctive	(io) faccia, (tu) faccia, (Lei) faccia, (lui / lei) faccia, (noi) facciamo, (voi) facciate, (loro) facciano
Imperfect Subjunctive	(io) facessi, (tu) facessi, (Lei) facesse, (lui / lei) facesse, (noi) facessimo, (voi) faceste, (loro) facessero
Gerund	facendo

leggere / to read

Past Participle	letto
Past Absolute	(io) lessi, (tu) leggesti, (Lei) lesse, (lui / lei) lesse, (noi) leggemmo, (voi) leggeste, (loro) lessero

mettere / to put

Past Participle	messo
Past Absolute	(io) misi, (tu) mettesti, (Lei) mise, (lui / lei) mise, (noi) mettemmo, (voi) metteste, (loro) misero

_morire_* / to die

Present Indicative	(io) muoio, (tu) muori, (Lei) muore, (lui / lei) muore, (noi) moriamo, (voi) morite, (loro) muoiono
Past Participle	morto
Present Subjunctive	(io) muoia, (tu) muoia, (Lei) muoia, (lui / lei) muoia, (noi) moriamo, (voi) morite, (loro) muoiano

_nascere_* / to be born

Past Participle	nato
Past Absolute	(io) nacqui, (tu) nascesti, (Lei) nacque, (lui / lei) nacque, (noi) nascemmo, (voi) nasceste, (loro) nacquero

perdere / to lose

Past Participle	perso
Past Absolute	(io) persi, (tu) perdesti, (Lei) perse, (lui / lei) perse, (noi) perdemmo, (voi) perdeste, (loro) persero

_piacere_* / to like, be pleasing to

Present Indicative	(io) piaccio, (tu) piaci, (Lei) piace, (lui / lei) piace, (noi) piacciamo, (voi) piacete, (loro) piacciono

| *Past Absolute* | (io) piacqui, (tu) piacesti, (Lei) piacque, (lui / lei) piacque, (noi) piacemmo, (voi) piaceste, (loro) piacquero |
| *Present Subjunctive* | (io) piaccia, (tu) piaccia, (Lei) piaccia, (lui / lei) piaccia, (noi) piacciamo, (voi) piacciate, (loro) piacciano |

<u>potere</u> / to be able to

Present Indicative	(io) posso, (tu) puoi, (Lei) può, (lui / lei) può, (noi) possiamo, (voi) potete, (loro) possono
Future	(io) potrò, (tu) potrai, (Lei) potrà, (lui / lei) potrà, (noi) potremo, (voi) potrete, (loro) potranno
Conditional	(io) potrei, (tu) potresti, (Lei) potrebbe, (lui / lei) potrebbe, (noi) potremmo, (voi) potreste, (loro) potrebbero
Present Subjunctive	(io) possa, (tu) possa, (Lei) possa, (lui / lei) possa, (noi) possiamo, (voi) possiate, (loro) possano

<u>prendere</u> / to take

| *Past Participle* | preso |
| *Past Absolute* | (io) presi, (tu) prendesti, (Lei) prese, (lui / lei) prese, (noi) prendemmo, (voi) prendeste, (loro) presero |

<u>salire</u> / to go up, climb

Present Indicative	(io) salgo, (tu) sali, (Lei) sale, (lui / lei) sale, (noi) saliamo, (voi) salite, (loro) salgono
Imperative	(tu) sali, (Lei) salga, (noi) saliamo, (voi) salite, (Loro) salgano
Present Subjunctive	(io) salga, (tu) salga, (Lei) salga, (lui / lei) salga, (noi) saliamo, (voi) saliate, (loro) salgano

sapere / to know

Present Indicative	(io) so, (tu) sai, (Lei) sa, (lui / lei) sa, (noi) sappiamo, (voi) sapete, (loro) sanno
Future	(io) saprò, (tu) saprai, (Lei) saprà, (lui / lei) saprà, (noi) sapremo, (voi) saprete, (loro) sapranno
Imperative	(tu) sappi, (Lei) sappia, (noi) sappiamo, (voi) sappiate, (Loro) sappiano
Conditional	(io) saprei, (tu) sapresti, (Lei) saprebbe, (lui / lei) saprebbe, (noi) sapremmo, (voi) sapreste, (loro) saprebbero
Present Subjunctive	(io) sappia, (tu) sappia, (Lei) sappia, (lui / lei) sappia, (noi) sappiamo, (voi) sappiate, (loro) sappiano

scegliere / to choose, select

Present Indicative	(io) scelgo, (tu) scegli, (Lei) sceglie, (lui / lei) sceglie, (noi) scegliamo, (voi) scegliete, (loro) scelgono
Past Participle	scelto
Past Absolute	(io) scelsi, (tu) scegliesti, (Lei) scelse, (lui / lei) scelse, (noi) scegliemmo, (voi) sceglieste, (loro) scelsero
Imperative	(tu) scegli, (Lei) scelga, (noi) scegliamo, (voi) scegliete, (Loro) scelgano
Present Subjunctive	(io) scelga, (tu) scelga, (Lei) scelga, (lui / lei) scelga, (noi) scegliamo, (voi) scegliate, (loro) scelgano

scendere / to descend, go down

Past Participle	sceso
Past Absolute	(io) scesi, (tu) scendesti, (Lei) scese, (lui / lei) scese, (noi) scendemmo, (voi) scendeste, (loro) scesero

scrivere / to write

Past Participle	scritto
Past Absolute	(io) scrissi, (tu) scrivesti, (Lei) scrisse, (lui / lei) scrisse, (noi) scrivemmo, (voi) scriveste, (loro) scrissero

_stare_* / to stay

Present Indicative	(io) sto, (tu) stai, (Lei) sta, (lui / lei) sta, (noi) stiamo, (voi) state, (loro) stanno
Past Participle	stato
Imperfect	(io) stavo, (tu) stavi, (Lei) stava, (lui / lei) stava, (noi) stavamo, (voi) stavate, (loro) stavano
Past Absolute	(io) stetti, (tu) stesti, (Lei) stette, (lui / lei) stette, (noi) stemmo, (voi) steste, (loro) stettero
Future	(io) starò, (tu) starai, (Lei) starà, (lui / lei) starà, (noi) staremo, (voi) starete, (loro) staranno
Imperative	(tu) sta', (Lei) stia, (noi) stiamo, (voi) state, (Loro) stiano
Conditional	(io) starei, (tu) staresti, (Lei) starebbe, (lui / lei) starebbe, (noi) staremmo, (voi) stareste, (loro) starebbero
Present Subjunctive	(io) stia, (tu) stia, (Lei) stia, (lui / lei) stia, (noi) stiamo, (voi) stiate, (loro) stiano
Imperfect Subjunctive	(io) stessi, (tu) stessi, (Lei) stesse, (lui / lei) stesse, (noi) stessimo, (voi) steste, (loro) stessero

tenere / to hold, keep

Present Indicative	(io) tengo, (tu) tieni, (Lei) tiene, (lui / lei) tiene, (noi) teniamo, (voi) tenete, (loro) tengono
Past Absolute	(io) tenni, (tu) tenesti, (Lei) tenne, (lui / lei) tenne, (noi) tenemmo, (voi) teneste, (loro) tennero

Future	(io) terrò, (tu) terrai, (Lei) terrà, (lui / lei) terrà, (noi) terremo, (voi) terrete, (loro) terranno
Imperative	(tu) tieni, (Lei) tenga, (noi) teniamo, (voi) tenete, (Loro) tengano
Conditional	(io) terrei, (tu) terresti, (Lei) terrebbe, (lui / lei) terrebbe, (noi) terremmo, (voi) terreste, (loro) terrebbero
Present Subjunctive	(io) tenga, (tu) tenga, (Lei) tenga, (lui / lei) tenga, (noi) teniamo, (voi) teniate, (loro) tengano

<u>uscire</u>* / to go out

Present Indicative	(io) esco, (tu) esci, (Lei) esce, (lui / lei) esce, (noi) usciamo, (voi) uscite, (loro) escono
Imperative	(tu) esci, (Lei) esca, (noi) usciamo, (voi) uscite, (Loro) escano
Present Subjunctive	(io) esca, (tu) esca, (Lei) esca, (lui / lei) esca, (noi) usciamo, (voi) usciate, (loro) escano

<u>vedere</u> / to see

Past Participle	visto/veduto
Past Absolute	(io) vidi, (tu) vedesti, (Lei) vide, (lui / lei) vide, (noi) vedemmo, (voi) vedeste, (loro) videro
Future	(io) vedrò, (tu) vedrai, (Lei) vedrà, (lui / lei) vedrà, (noi) vedremo, (voi) vedrete, (loro) vedranno
Conditional	(io) vedrei, (tu) vedresti, (Lei) vedrebbe, (lui / lei) vedrebbe, (noi) vedremmo, (voi) vedreste, (loro) vedrebbero

<u>venire</u>* / to come

| *Present Indicative* | (io) vengo, (tu) vieni, (Lei) viene, (lui / lei) viene, (noi) veniamo, (voi) venite, (loro) vengono |

Past Participle	venuto
Past Absolute	(io) venni, (tu) venisti, (Lei) venne, (lui / lei) venne, (noi) venimmo, (voi) veniste, (loro) vennero
Future	(io) verrò, (tu) verrai, (Lei) verrà, (lui / lei) verrà, (noi) verremo, (voi) verrete, (loro) verranno
Imperative	(tu) vieni, (Lei) venga, (noi) veniamo, (voi) venite, (Loro) vengano
Conditional	(io) verrei, (tu) verresti, (Lei) verrebbe, (lui / lei) verrebbe, (noi) verremmo, (voi) verreste, (loro) verrebbero
Present Subjunctive	(io) venga, (tu) venga, (Lei) venga, (lui / lei) venga, (noi) veniamo, (voi) veniate, (loro) vengano

<u>volere</u> / to want

Present Indicative	(io) voglio, (tu) vuoi, (Lei) vuole, (lui / lei) vuole, (noi) vogliamo, (voi) volete, (loro) vogliono
Past Absolute	(io) volli, (tu) volesti, (Lei) volle, (lui / lei) volle, (noi) volemmo, (voi) voleste, (loro) vollero
Future	(io) vorrò, (tu) vorrai, (Lei) vorrà, (lui / lei) vorrà, (noi) vorremo, (voi) vorrete, (loro) vorranno
Conditional	(io) vorrei, (tu) vorresti, (Lei) vorrebbe, (lui / lei) vorrebbe, (noi) vorremmo, (voi) vorreste, (loro) vorrebbero
Present Subjunctive	(io) voglia, (tu) voglia, (Lei) voglia, (lui / lei) voglia, (noi) vogliamo, (voi) vogliate, (loro) vogliano

Index

The items in this index that refer to topics in *The Basics*, *Parts of Speech*, and *Special Topics* sections are indicated by the § symbol. References to verbs in the *Verb Charts* section are indicated by page number (p.).

AT A GLANCE Series

Barron's new series gives travelers instant access to the most common idiomatic expressions used during a trip—the kind one needs to know instantly, like "Where can I find a taxi?" and "How much does this cost?"

Organized by situation (arrival, customs, hotel, health, etc.) and containing additional information about pronunciation, grammar, shopping plus special facts about the country, these convenient, pocket-size reference books will be the tourist's most helpful guides.

Special features include a bilingual dictionary section with over 2000 key words, maps of each country and major cities, and helpful phonetic spellings throughout.

Each book paperback, 256 pp., 3¾" x 6"

ARABIC AT A GLANCE, Wise (0-7641-1248-1) $8.95, Can. $12.50
CHINESE AT A GLANCE, Seligman & Chen (0-7641-1250-3) $8.95, Can. $12.50
FRENCH AT A GLANCE, 4th, Stein & Wald (0-7641-2512-5) $6.95, Can. $9.95
GERMAN AT A GLANCE, 4th, Strutz (0-7641-2516-8) $6.95, Can. $9.95
ITALIAN AT A GLANCE, 4th, Costantino (0-7641-2513-3) $6.95, Can. $9.95
JAPANESE AT A GLANCE, 3rd, Akiyama (0-7641-0320-2) $8.95, Can. $11.95
KOREAN AT A GLANCE, Holt (0-8120-3998-X) $8.95, Can. $11.95
RUSSIAN AT A GLANCE, Beyer (0-7641-1251-1) $8.95, Can. $12.50
SPANISH AT A GLANCE, 4th, Wald (0-7641-2514-1) $6.95, Can. $9.95

Barron's Educational Series, Inc.
250 Wireless Blvd., Hauppauge, NY 11788
Call toll-free: 1-800-645-3476
In Canada: Georgetown Book Warehouse, 34 Armstrong Ave.
Georgetown, Ont. L7G 4R9, Call toll-free: 1-800-247-7160
Visit our website at: www.barronseduc.com

Books may be purchased at your bookstore, or by mail from Barron's. Enclose check or money order for total amount plus sales tax where applicable and 18% for postage and handling (minimum charge $5.95). NY State and California residents add sales tax. Prices subject to change without notice.
Can. $ = Canadian dollars
(#25) R 3/04